W9-BCZ-149

B&T
$8.95

THE DISCOVERY OF
BANGLADESH

DISCOVERY OF BANGLADESH

THE BOOK IS DEDICATED TO THE MEMORY OF ABOUT A MILLION WHO FELL VICTIM TO THE NATURAL CYCLONE DISASTER OF NOVEMBER 1970, AND TO THREE MILLIONS WHO WITHIN A FEW WEEKS OF THE FOLLOWING YEAR WERE ORPHANED, WIDOWED, RAPED, BUTCHERED WHILE ASLEEP, AND MOWED DOWN ON THE STREETS THROUGH NO FAULT OF THEIR OWN.

THE DISCOVERY OF BANGLADESH

BY

STEPHEN M. GILL

MELKSHAM

COLIN VENTON

Wingate College Library

ISBN 0 85475 106 8

COPYRIGHT NOTICE

© STEPHEN M. GILL MCMLXXV

75-330161 Oct 4, 1976

All rights reserved. No part of this publication
may be reproduced, stored in a retrieval
system, or transmitted, in any form or by any
means, electronic or otherwise, without the prior
permission of Colin Venton Limited.

Set 11 on 12 point Intertype Baskerville
and printed in Great Britain
at the Press of the Publisher,
The Uffington Press,
Melksham, Wiltshire,
SN12 6LA (U.K.).

LIST OF CONTENTS

067665

LIST OF ILLUSTRATIONS

Photos numbers 6, 7, 8, 10, 12, 14 and 16 by courtesy of the Indian Government.

MY GOLDEN BENGAL

O my golden Bengal, I love thee :
Always your sky and your wind play music in my heart.
O mother, the fragrance of spring in your mango-forests
    makes me wild with joy.
And in your rich autumn fields I have seen your smile, so
    sweet.

What beauty and shade, what affection and tenderness
    have you spread—
In the shadows of your trees, in the banks of your rivers.
O mother, your words sound heavenly in my ears;
And when your face is sad, my eyes fill with tears.

My childhood has passed in your playroom;
And blessed am I, covered with your dust and earth.
O mother, at the end of day when you light your lamps,
I leave my play and run back to you.

All my life I have spent
In your pastures and ferry-ghats,
In your village-roads full of shade and the songs of birds,
In your courtyards laden with rice.
O mother, your peasants and farmers are my brothers, my
    own.

Here I am, my mother, my head at your feet.
Let the dust from your feet be the gem on my forehead.
O mother, my meagre fortunes, I lay before your feet;
And jewels from others I shall never buy
For they soon become a noose round your neck.

(Rabindranath Tagore)

Mohammad Ali Jinnah
the founder of Pakistan

Sheikh Mujibur Rahman
Prime Minister
The People's Republic of Bangladesh

Mr. Justice Abu Sayed Chowdhury
President
The People's Republic of Bangladesh

ACKNOWLEDGEMENTS

THE writer gratefully acknowledges those authors, periodicals, magazines and publishers to whom he is indebted for quotations. Credit is given to them in the proper places.

The writer gratefully acknowledges also the following individuals and libraries:

Mr. R. N. Nath, Public Relations Officer of the India High Commission in Canada; Mr. Abdul Momin, High Commissioner for Bangladesh in Canada; Mr. Jamil Majid, third secretary of Bangladesh Embassy in Canada; and Mr. Tipu Sultan—for their useful suggestions, comments, pictures, clippings of various periodicals and magazines and some important books concerning Bangladesh.

Mr. Gordon Ferris, the author's friend, who read critically a part of the manuscript.

Simon Fraser Library of Cornwall, Ontario, for quick arrangement of books through the inter-library loan; and The National Archives, Ottawa.

Stephen M. Gill

11

PREFACE

by

SENATOR PAUL YUZYK, Ph.D.,

University of Ottawa

THE people of the world followed with alarm and dismay on television and radio and in the newspapers the tragic events of 1971 as they unfolded in a region which was known as East Pakistan. Out of this confusion and the atrocities which were perpetrated by a dictatorial government on virtually a defenceless people, there emerged a new nation and a new country of some 75,000,000 population — Bangladesh. Millions of the best sons and daughters perished, some of which we saw on film and in photographs, to give birth to the independence of their nation and to a new and better life for the people. This is a dramatic story.

Those of us who were far removed from the tragic scene of action saw it happen in a limited way but we could not always understand the forces that helped to shape the course of events. We could only hope that a historian would undertake to write an authentic account and bring to light as much truth as possible so that we would understand the aspirations of a brave people who fought, suffered and shed their precious blood for freedom and democracy.

12

A reputable poet, sensitive to the anguishes of the oppressed and suffering human being offered his talent to write this moving story. Stephen M. Gill the poet became the narrator and the historian to give us a fuller understanding of the victory of this new nation.

For many of the readers this historical account will indeed be the *Discovery of Bangladesh,* as the title implies. The experience of this discovery will undoubtedly make the reader re-assess human values, his role in life and in the world. The problems of Bangladesh are also the problems of the world and their solution should help stabilize humanity. The United Nations must be made a more effective instrument to realize and maintain justice, peace, progress and prosperity on a world-wide scale.

Stephen Gill put his heart and his scholarly training into the task to produce a manuscript which is basically factual and comprehensible, yet presented in an interesting manner. The story of Bangladesh is related chronologically, the chief causes are explained, the important personalities are vividly portrayed, the role of the world powers with emphasis on India is made apparent and the documentation and bibliography are provided. Much useful information about the people, the country, the resources, the culture, the economic development and potentialities as well as prospects is brought together. It is not only a history but also a handbook, essential to the understanding of the new state.

One wonders what will be the fate of Bangladesh. The forces of freedom and democracy have triumphed at a great sacrifice and cost, which has won the admiration of all people in the world who believe in this cause. Will India be the only democratic state to provide assistance to the new nation? Should not the other democratic states of the world not feel the same responsibility? Their response will be the test of the survival of democracy on this earth.

13

Wingate College Library

INTRODUCTION

Discovery of Bangladesh is a story of untold sufferings and patience, and of characteristic features of a people who have played and have yet to play a significant role in the world politics. Bangladesh, a nation of seventy-five million people, has faced one of the greatest tragedies of the human race; little is known of Bangladesh and its tragedy by the contemporary readers. Many of those who claim to know Bangladesh have formed their opinions on the basis of scattered and scanty knowledge gleaned from the news media. Others find themselves caught in a maze in the absence of a guide which can offer them information dispassionately. The present study is designed to fill this vacuum in the sincere hope that it will meet the needs of those who want to know of a nation which is young in some aspects, old in others, but always fascinating. To achieve this purpose the author has tried to be as objective as it is humanly possible.

The subject is treated in three main parts. The first part is a historical survey of the emergence of a new nation; the second part is about the land, and its inhabitants in general; and the third part includes some basic facts, a chronology of important dates, bibliography for further reading, and index.

The author has explored every possible source to make it a competent work. The book's three chapters entitled "Causes of Friction", "Demand for Autonomy" and "Political Parties" have appeared in the *Canadian India Times*. Some material for other chapters was used by the author in a speech broadcast on CJSS radio station, Cornwall, Canada, and for an interview he gave on the Cablevision Eleven.

PART I

EMERGENCE OF BANGLADESH

1—HISTORICAL BACKGROUND

THE region known as Bangladesh came into existence in 1947—at the time when India was divided to establish a new nation, Pakistan. This region was carved out of the eastern part of Bengal, a province which ever remained a part of India. In 1947, eastern Bengal was linked with Pakistan and was called East Pakistan. When it achieved its independence from West Pakistan in 1971, its people officially adopted the name of Bangladesh for their country. It is obvious that before 1971 Bangladesh had never the status of a nation. Its people and the people of West Bengal, which is still a province of India, speak the same language, have the same food habits, have the same attitude towards life, they look alike and have a common historical background. Therefore any attempt to trace Bangladesh's past will lead to the past of the undivided Bengal.

The history of its people before the third century, B.C., is obscure, though it is said that the word Bengal is derived from the ancient kingdom of "Banga" mentioned first in the Sanskrit literature thousands of years ago. It is also said that ethnically, Austro-Asians and a section of the Dravadians from west of India formed the early population of this land. A small portion of the Aryans, when they arrived in India, might have migrated there. There was also a great influx of the Mongolians from Tibet and

16

Plate 1—Ralindramate Tagare.

Plate 2—Shops on the main Kushtia highway practically levelled by Pakistani fire.

Burma. Later came the Arabs, the Persians, the Turks, and the Afghans. All of them integrated themselves with the natives.

In the third century, B.C., Bengal formed a part of the Maurya empire inherited by Asoka, a great emperor of India. From the 8th to the 12th century it remained a part of the domain of the Buddhist Pala kings of northern India. From the 13th century to the middle of the 18th century the land was ruled by various Muslim conquerors. During this period many Hindus accepted Islam. The Muslim religion, unlike in other parts of the sub-continent, did not spread here through force and violence. It was spread rather by saints who came to India to seek truth. It has been noted that at the time of Fakhruddin, a ruler, there were around 150 Muslim saints in Bengal itself.

Aliverdi Khan, almost an adventurer, seized Bengal in 1740. He could be considered the last Muslim ruler of the province. At that time Bengal was still a rich part of India; it produced cotton, silk and saltpeter in abundance. Bengal's rivers provided cheap means of transport. Aliverdi Khan died in April 1756. After his death his domain was beset with internal problems. His successors were young, inexperienced and blinded with family jealousies. At that time the East India Company, a well-known British concern, enjoyed wide trade monopolies there and therefore the company was in an advantageous position to manoeuvre the chaotic political situation in its favour, which it did by using all means possible. As a result, the British established a firm hold over Bengal after defeating the successor of Aliverdi Khan in 1757 in the famous battle of Plassey. The British placed Bengal under a governor-general and made Calcutta, a Hindu-dominated area, its capital.

In the British period, the Hindus dominated the cultural and economic activities. Under Lord Cornwallis the zamindar (feudal) system was built; this made many Hindus

17   2

feudal lords, though a few Muslims were also benefited from this system. Since the Muslims suffered economically, they remained a backward class. In dealing with Hindus, their superiors in economic fields, they faced humiliation and after the formation of Pakistan they were again humiliated at the hands of West Pakistanis. They rid themselves of these centuries-old humiliations in 1971 when they succeeded in forming a sovereign democratic government.

After independence, Bangladesh became a synonym for abject poverty. There is much evidence to attest the good old days of this new nation of Muslim Bengalees. A number of times European travellers of past have mentioned this territory in their accounts. In his book, *An Economic Geography of East Pakistan,* Mr. Nafis Ahmad has quoted many times from the original writings of these travellers. He says that "travellers like Iben Battuta (1345), Marco Polo, the Chinese Mahuan (1406), the Italian Lewis Vertomannus, Caesar Frederick (1565-81) and Ralph Fitch (1582-83) and others, and all Muslim historians, corroborate the story of East Pakistan's (now Bangladesh) matchless fertility, abundance and prosperity."[1]

According to the archeological discoveries, the city of Mahasthan in Bogra, called Pundranagar in olden days, is the oldest one. It appears to have remained the provincial capital of several Hindu dynasties. This and other discoveries found in Dinajpur, in Rajshahi, and in the southern part of the country speak highly of the glorious past of the nation.

---

[1]Nafis Ahmad, *An Economic Geography of East Pakistan* (Oxford, 1968), p. 75.

2—FORMATION OF PAKISTAN

HISTORY will tell that the British extended their reign in India through their policy of divide and rule. In 1932, they introduced into Indian politics the Communal Award; according to this the members of provincial and national assemblies represented only their respective religions. Before the British came, India had been ruled by Hindu and Muslim kings. Communal riots were unknown in those days. Riots stemmed from the British policy of dividing the Indians on the basis of their religious creed. The Communal Award created dissension among the followers of the different religions, particularly between the Hindus and the Muslims.

The Muslim League, a political party which claimed to represent Muslims, fought in its initial stages to defend the rights and privileges of Muslims in unified India. Gradually, under the leadership of Mohammad Ali Jinnah, the Muslim League demanded a separate territory for Muslims on the ground that Muslims form a different race from the rest of the Indians and that in such a territory they would preserve their culture, traditions, prosper economically, and live according to their Islamic principles. They called this territory Pakistan, which means a land of pure, or holy people. It is said that the word Pakistan was coined and first used in England.

The National Congress, a representative party of Indians of all castes and creeds, stood against the idea of partition for the simple reason that its leaders foresaw a threat to the integrity and strength of India in the acceptance of a theory they thought absurd and baseless.

This conflict between the major political parties gave the British Government an opportunity to prolong their hold over India on the pretext that there was none to whom they could hand over the power. The leaders of the National Congress, Gandhi and Jawaharlal Nehru, were bent upon freeing India from the British rule as soon as possible. These leaders had no alternative, but to yield to Mr. Mohammad Ali Jinnah's demand; as a result of which the British Government passed a declaration on June 3, 1947, to divide India into two parts—India and Pakistan.

It was proposed that representatives of the Punjab and Bengal provinces in the Provincial Assemblies would decide their future by a simple majority vote; the Legislative Assembly of Sind province would vote as a whole on the issue; the Northwest Frontier province and Sylhet district of Assam would have a referendum; Baluchistan would decide through a joint meeting of its representative institutions.

Leaders of the National Congress and of the Muslim League consented to these proposals. As was expected, the provinces of the Northwest Frontier, Sind, Baluchistan and the Sylhet district of Assam voted for Pakistan. The provinces of the Punjab and Bengal were divided—western part of the Punjab and eastern part of Bengal became part of Pakistan. Some of the states also joined Pakistan. Territorial division was followed by a division of military forces and armaments.

The whole procedure used to divide India was undemocratic. In Baluchistan, for instance, no election was held. In other provinces only those who were granted the right

20

to vote under the 1935 Constitution voted. Because of this Constitution in certain provinces such as Northwest Frontier only 15 per cent of the population had the right to vote.

Partition was followed by communal riots. About 12 million people suffered and a million were killed. Many Muslims were against partition. Nearly all the Hindus, Sikhs, Christians, and followers of other religions were also against it. Some of the Muslim League leaders, who formerly advocated partition, began to sense dangers in the partition of Bengal. Suhrawardy, a Muslim League leader from East Bengal, or East Pakistan now Bangladesh, tried to stop it on the eve of partition; he wanted independence for the whole province of Bengal. Some suggested a referendum should be held to solve the problem of Bengal. It is said that the people of Bengal did not want the partition of their province.

However, Pakistan came into existence on 14th August, 1947. On the recommendation of the Muslim League, the king of England appointed Mr. Mohammad Ali Jinnah as the first Governor General of Pakistan. Mr. Liaquat Ali Khan, who served Muslim League's secretary, became the Prime Minister. Pakistan decided to remain in the British Commonwealth.

3—EAST PAKISTAN AND WEST PAKISTAN

EAST BENGAL and Sylhet district of Assam formed East Pakistan, and the provinces of Sind, Baluchistan, the Northwest Frontier, West Punjab and some States comprised West Pakistan. East and West Pakistan were separated by 1,200 miles of land and 2,500 miles of sea. This 1,200 miles of territory belongs to India. Until February 1971, Pakistani aeroplanes used to cross this Indian land in three hours to reach Dacca, the capital of East Pakistan, from Karachi (West Pakistan). In February 1971 an Indian aircraft was hijacked to Lahore, West Pakistan, where it was set on fire. After this incident, the Indian Government banned flights of Pakistani aeroplanes over India; they had to fly via Colombo, Ceylon, and thus had to cover 2,400 miles to reach the other wing of Pakistan. It is possible to travel by sea from Karachi to Chittagong (a port of East Pakistan); it takes about eleven days by sea. This was a peculiar situation unlikely to be found in any other country of the world.

Fifty million West Pakistanis consist of four major ethnic groups: Punjabis, Pakhtuns, Sindhis, and Baluchis. Each of these groups has its own language and way of life. On the other hand, 75 million Bengalees comprise 98 per cent of the population in East Pakistan. Bengalees have one language and are proud of their ancestry; their language and literature are older than Urdu, the national language of Pakistan, used by minority.

The east is almost entirely alluvial, humid, and gets excessive rains. It produces crops such as rice, tea, jute, which are not cultivated in West Pakistan as these plants need plenty of water. West Pakistan produces wheat, millet and cotton, crops which do not require much water.

West Pakistan covers a greater area, a substantial part of which is mountainous. The east, a smaller area, has a denser population. According to the 1951 census 55.5 per cent of the whole population of both the wings lived in East Pakistan.

Both the wings of Pakistan were split not only geographically, but in nearly everything except in their religion. People of Bangladesh are different from the people of the West Pakistan, historically, economically, and ethnically. They use different costume, have different food habits, different language, different standard time, even their outlook towards life is different. Their ties with West Pakistan were so unnatural that even at the time of partition there were rumours that East Bengal would soon secede from Pakistan and become a part of India again. These rumours subsided for some time after partition, but West Pakistan's misgiving about the people of East Pakistan never abated. Whenever there was any movement or demonstration they suspected it was engineered by the Indian spies and agents.

Pakistan is unique in the sense that it is perhaps the only country which emerged from religious feelings. Pakistan was created on the assumption that Muslims would receive better treatment by their own brothers in their own country; this illusion was dispelled when Muslims started exploiting and killing other Muslims. In West Pakistan there were riots between the major sects of their religion. In the name of God and Muslim unity, West Pakistan exploited the people of East Pakistan for 24 years, treating

23

it as a colony. A continuous tension between both the wings has proved that geographical unity and a common cultural heritage are stronger ties than religion, which these days has become a personal matter. Had a common religion been the basis of unity, the Pakistani rulers would have given equal opportunities to all parts of their country to prosper. As a matter of fact, religion has never been a complete unifying force in history. Had it been the case nearly all Europe would have become united long ago; the United States, Canada and some other Christian countries of North America would have formed one government; and all the Muslim countries of the world would have become one nation. Muslim history is packed with incidents when Muslims plundered and murdered other Muslims. Christian and Hindu histories are also packed with similar incidents.

4—CAUSES OF FRICTION

Towards the end of the first chapter mention was made that certain leaders, notably Suhrawardy, a Muslim League leader, foresaw dangers in the division of Bengal. None cared to listen to them. As anticipated, the consequences of partition began to manifest themselves in the very first year of Pakistan's life. East Bengal began to feel that West Pakistan was treating her as a colony. This gradually drove almost the whole of its populace along the road to a long, bloody strife.

The following are considered the reasons which compelled East Pakistan to sever its ties with Pakistan and establish a Sovereign Democratic Republic of Bangladesh :

1. Since Bengalees comprised 56 per cent of the total population of both the wings of Pakistan, they wanted their language, Bengali, to be the official language. Instead, at the time Pakistan was formed, Urdu was imposed as the official language.

2. Sixty per cent of the country's budget was used for defence, out of which only 10 per cent was made available to the people of Bangladesh. Defence services were kept for the West Pakistanis, who filled 90 per cent of the positions in the Armed Forces.

3. The senior military staff of the administration were all from West Pakistan.

4. The Army Headquarters were established in West Pakistan, whereas the majority of the population lived in East Pakistan.

5. Eighty-five per cent of positions in the civil service were filled by West Pakistanis.

6. In the Central Government 80 per cent jobs were given to the people from the western wing. The west monopolized such positions as of secretaries and of joint secretaries. The Deputy Chairman of the Planning Commission and the Central Finance Minister, key positions to allocate resources, were always held by West Pakistanis.

7. Eighty per cent of the foreign exchange was earned by the produce of Bangladesh—tea and jute. This foreign exchange was utilized by West Pakistan to hire technical experts from abroad and to buy vital machinery and raw material for their region.

8. West Pakistanis employed a unique method to exploit the people of Bangladesh. Whatever machinery Bangladesh needed, West Pakistan bought it from foreign countries. It was then sold to the people of Bangladesh at two or three times the purchase price. West Pakistanis demanded this price in sterling, American dollars and francs. Even the local produce of West Pakistan was sold to the eastern wing for foreign currency. As a result, Bangladesh suffered loss in its trade with West Pakistan and became poorer.

9. The Pakistan Industrial Credit and Investment Corporation, and The Industrial Development Bank of Pakistan allocated far less in loans to Bangladesh than to West Pakistan.

10. In the utilization of loans, West Pakistan used to spend larger portions because the western zone received better facilities from the Central Government to make use of those loans. Bangladesh could use only the minimum, sometimes even less than 50 per cent of its total allocated

loans.

11. Due to the unfair policy of the west wing, Bangladesh always had a shortage of food. To keep the feudal lords happy and contented, no attempt was made to solve the agrarian problems.

12. There always was a great disparity in income between both the regions. In 1949-50 per capita income of West Pakistan exceeded that of East Pakistan by 9 per cent. This figure rose to 30 per cent by 1959-60, 40 per cent by 1964-65 and 60 per cent by 1969-70. On the other hand, conditions in Bangladesh remained stagnant due to the injust economic policy of the Central Government.

13. Eighty per cent of the foreign aid received from the World Bank and other countries was spent on West Pakistan and Bangladesh received only 20 per cent of this aid.

14. Prices in Bangladesh were always higher than in West Pakistan. Rice, wheat, mustard oil, requirements of everyday life, were always expensive in the eastern wing. *Pacific Affairs* of June 1955 confirmed it.

15. According to the *Dawn,* Karachi, July 13, 1953, jute sown by East Bengalees without permission of the Government was destroyed. It led to waste and discontentment among the farmers of Bangladesh.

16. Most of the mill owners in the eastern wing are from West Pakistan. These mill owners got raw material from the Government at a lower price. But Bengalee craftsmen and owners of small-scale industries had to purchase raw material on the black market, for which they had to pay 20 to 30 per cent more than the actual price. This affected their profits. Many of them had to close down their business. West Pakistanis, owners of most of the mills, having the support of the Government, flourished.

27

17. There was a wide gap in salaries between the East and West Pakistani employees. The West Pakistani capitalists, who own their businesses in the eastern wing, pay higher salaries to workers from their part of the country. The employees from the East Pakistan received about half the wages of what Pakistanis from the west get.

18. Bangladesh essentially remained an agricultural country, a producer of raw material for West Pakistan. From the raw material produced in Bangladesh, West Pakistan earned more foreign exchange which they used for their benefit only.

19. The constant tension between both the wings of Pakistan and the continuous unstable conditions were the factors responsible for the Bengalee businessmen's fear of investing their capital in big industries. Rich Hindu families deposited their money in banks in India or in England.

The following tables manifest the extent of disparity between both the wings of Pakistan :

TABLE 1
Education : 1965-1966

Institution	Number in Bangladesh	Number in West Pakistan
Secondary Vocational School	17	34
Teachers' Training Institute	59	87
University	4	6
Affiliated Colleges:		
a. Engineering	1	7
b. Medical	7	9
c. Law	5	8
d. Commerce	2	5
e. Agricultural	1	4

(Source : 20 Years of Pakistan in Statistics, C.S.O.)

TABLE 2

Health : 1966

Institution	Number in Bangladesh	Number in West Pakistan
Hospitals	76	393
Dispensaries	489	1754
Beds in Hospitals and Dispensaries	6984	26200
Population/Bed Ratio	9000 : 1	2000 : 1

(Source: 20 Years of Pakistan in Statistics, C.S.O.)

TABLE 3

Languages Used in Pakistan

Languages	Pakistan	East Pakistan (Bangladesh)	West Pakistan
Bengali	55.48	98.42	0.12
Punjabi	29.02	0.02	66.39
Pushto	3.70	0.01	8.47
Sindhi	5.51	0.01	12.59
Baluchi	1.09	——	2.49
Urdu	3.65	0.61	7.57

(Source: Pakistan Year Book 1969.)
Note: Figures show percentage.

5—DEMAND FOR AUTONOMY

For 24 years East Pakistan was treated by West Pakistanis as their colony. During this time many rulers came and went away—Mohammad Ali Jinnah, Iskander Mirza, Ayub Khan and last of all Yahya Khan were virtually dictators who stifled the voice of majority, exploited them, and suppressed their demands with the help of military. They ruled Pakistan in the name of Muslim unity and God, and kept refusing, on one pretext or another, the people's right to govern themselves through their elected representatives. Whenever East Pakistan asked for autonomy they were silenced with might. Not only East Pakistan demanded autonomy, the provinces of Baluchistan and Northwest Frontier desired it too. About 60 per cent of the entire population of both the wings and almost all from East Pakistan clamoured for self-rule.

In 1929, a Conference of all the Muslim political parties was convened by Mohammad Shafi and Liaquat Ali Khan in Delhi. The Conference, presided over by Agha Khan, discussed Mohammad Ali Jinnah's fourteen points, later submitted to the Round Table Conference of 1930. The first two points of Mr. Jinnah, the founder of Pakistan, concerned the political arrangement of Pakistan after the freedom and division of India. It recommended a federal government with autonomous provinces for the forthcoming Islamic state. All the Muslim parties approved these points.

Eleven years after this Conference and seven years before Pakistan came into existence, the Muslim League's All-India session was held at Lahore on March 20-23, 1940. In this session the Muslim League reiterated its demand for the division of India on religious grounds. Mr. Mohammad Ali Jinnah, in his presidential speech, emphasized that Indian Muslims, who are concentrated mostly in the eastern and northwestern parts of the country, comprise a nation—not a communal group. As they form a separate nation they should be given a portion of India in which they may establish an Islamic state, their homeland. The provinces with Muslim majority should be integrated with the Islamic state, and in internal matters these provinces should be autonomous and sovereign. Soon after this session Mr. Jinnah, in his letter to Mahatama Gandhi, wrote that the National Congress should accept the Muslim League's demand for an Islamic country which would be governed by a government of the elected representatives of the people. He offered the Muslim League's full support to the National Congress in its fight for freedom if the latter acknowledges the Muslim League's demands. At this session a resolution, moved by then Chief Minister of united Bengal, Mr. A. K. Fazlul Haq, was passed. It reads as follows:

That geographically contiguous units be demarcated into regions which should be constituted with such territorial readjustments as may be necessary that the area in which the Muslims are numerically in a majority as in the North-Western and Eastern zones of India should be grouped to constitute Independent States in which the constituent units shall be autonomous and sovereign.[2]

The terms of this Lahore Resolution were clarified by Mr. Jinnah "in an interview which he gave to the Associated Press of America. Pakistan was to be a democratic

31

federal state comprising the existing provinces of the Northwest Frontier, Baluchistan, Sind and the Punjab in the west; and Bengal and Assam in the east."[3]

Mr. Leonard Binder in his book *Religion and Politics in Pakistan* makes an interesting point when he says that in the Lahore Resolution the word Pakistan was not used at all. The Muslim political parties backed Mr. Jinnah's fight for a separate state for they were given to understand that they will have independent states, autonomous and sovereign.[4]

Until the Lahore Resolution, the Muslim League was not popular among the Muslim masses; its influence was confined to intellectuals, landlords, and the merchant class. After this resolution was passed, the Muslim League began to exploit the religious sentiments of the working class. The Muslim League won their support.

At the time of partition some provinces such as the eastern part of Bengal voted for Muslim League because they envisaged the implementation of the Lahore Resolution. The British Government handed over her power to the Muslim League. Mr. Mohammad Ali Jinnah was appointed Governor General of Pakistan on the recommendation of his party. He became almost a dictator. He had vast power in his hands. The Lahore Resolution was completely ignored. Pakistan was equated with West Pakistan. A reign of suppression, terrorism, and of ignoble rule over East Pakistan was launched. Their language, their culture, their economy, their wishes and aspirations began to be curbed and crushed.

East Pakistan's demand for autonomy was not a whim of some of its leaders—rather it was a resolution, a firm determination of its people. The election of 1971, the first democratic election held since the birth of Pakistan, was fought on this issue and the Awami League party won a landslide victory. Obviously, the demand for autonomy

32

Plate 3—Houses in Dinajpur in Bangladesh razed to the ground by Pakistan shelling.

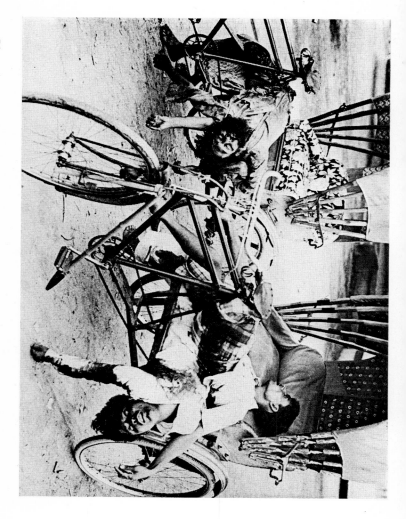

Plate 4—Cycle rickshaw pullers and passengers shot dead by Pakistani troops.

of the masses of East Pakistan was within the framework of the policy on which Pakistan was founded.

---

[2]*Bangladesh*: *Contemporary Events and Documents* (People's Republic of Bangladesh, 1971), p. 1.

[3]Richard Symonds, *The Making of Pakistan* (London, 1950), p. 62.

[4]Leonard Binder, *Religion and Politics in Pakistan* (Berkely and Los Angeles), p. 62.

3

6—POLITICAL PARTIES

IT HAS been seen in the first chapter that Muslim League, a political party based on religion, brought Pakistan into existence. After Pakistan's formation the people of the east began to realize that in the name of Religion they are being cheated. This awareness of the masses gave a death blow to the Muslim League. In the provincial election of 1954, the United Front, a coalition among various political parties, gave it a crushing defeat. The leaders of the West Pakistan could not tolerate this humiliation of the party which made Pakistan. They dismissed the Assembly of the coalition government and proclaimed the governor's rule in East Pakistan.

The Awami League—in English, People's League— emerged the leading political party of the east. It was formed after the partition to oppose the non-representative ruling party, the Muslim League. In the beginning this party in opposition was called Jinnah Awami Muslim League. In 1955, it dropped the names of Jinnah and Muslim to attract non-Muslims into its fold. The Awami League soon grew popular among the Bengalee masses. Under the leadership of Husain Shaheed Suhrawardy, it published its manifesto in 1952. The manifesto included the following points:

1. Taxes should be reduced in certain cases.
2. Higher taxes should be imposed on higher salaries.
3. No one should be allowed to keep more than 250

acres of land. Any land more than 250 acres should be taken away by the government with reasonable compensation paid to the owners.

4. The acquired land should be given to landless labourers for cultivation.

5. The country should be industrialized.

6. Corruptions like bribery, blackmarketing, favouritism should be stopped.

7. The political system should be democratized.

8. The non-representative Constitutional Assembly should be dissolved.

9. The Government should pursue a better foreign policy.

In January 1953, Ganatantri Dal—in English, Democratic Party—was born. Its leader Mohammad Ali was a left wing politician. The party aimed at achieving a democratic federal republic for Pakistan and full autonomy and equality for East Pakistan. It demanded abolition of feudal property, withdrawal of Pakistan from the British Commonwealth, and adoption of a neutral independent foreign policy. The Ganatantri Dal denounced communalism and opened its doors to the followers of any religion. It became a representative party of the progressive intelligensia of the east.

In the summer of 1953, Fazlul Haq, a veteran politician, laid the foundation of the Krishak Sramik (peasants and workers) Party. He was Advocate General of East Bengal, a post from which he resigned to form this party. The Krishak Sramik stood for the attainment of full autonomy for the provinces within Pakistan. The party's first conference was held in Dacca on July 26, 1953. Fazlul Haq was elected as its chairman and was given power to nominate the members of its Working Committee. Like the Awami League and Ganatantri Dal, its members are against communalism.

Fazlul Haq is the one who supported the Lahore Resolution of 1940, discussed in the previous chapter. In 1937, he headed the coalition government of Bengal province. His political party, Krishak Sramik, embodied its policy in twelve points. Important ones stress the demand for autonomy for the east as envisaged in the Lahore Resolution, recognition of Bengali as a provincial language, release of political prisoners and separation of judiciary from the executive powers.

From the parties discussed so far, the Ganatantri Dal and the Krishak Sramik were born and flourished in the east. On the other hand, the Awami League had its branches and membership in some parts of West Pakistan.

The National Awami League—in English, National People's Party—had its members in the east as well as in the west. In Bangladesh its influence is confined to some trade unions and peasants. But most of its supporters, students and peasants, live in West Pakistan. It did not participate in the December 1970 election, for its leaders were convinced that the military would never give up its power to the people's elected representatives. General Yahya Khan banned this political party on the pretext that it was planning to topple his military government.

The National Awami Party is split into two parts: pro-Peking and pro-Moscow groups. The pro-Moscow group believes that socialism must be achieved through democratic means, whereas the pro-Peking group advocates violence and force. Maulana Bhashani, an eighty-six-year-old, leads the pro-Moscow group in Bangladesh. Formerly, he was a Maoist. On Ayub Khan's advice, when he was the president of Pakistan, Maulana Bhashani led a delegation to communist China. After December 1970 elections he switched his sympathies to democratic methods to attain socialism. He wanted the world to forget his past. He tried hard to get arms from the Indian government to

36

drive out the West Pakistani forces. He often went to India for this purpose. It is difficult to tell if he could succeed in his mission. It is stated that his 55,000 well-organized peasants put up a hard fight against the Pakistani military. Since the beginning of the liberation war most of the prominent leaders of his group went underground to escape arrest and to carry on their activities and sabotage.

Mohammad Toha heads the communist party—Marxist-Leninist—in the Jessore area. Until 1969, he was a secretary of the National Awami Party. Mr. Toha, a well-educated man, is in his forties. His party is very small in size, but extremely well-organized. He is a Maoist in his ideology.

Among other small political parties are the National Congress, representative of most of the Hindus; the Nizam-i-Islam, representative of orthodox Muslim scholars; the Youth League, representative of students; the United Progressive Party; and the Scheduled Castes Federation.

7—RULE BEFORE FIELD-MARSHAL AYUB KHAN

(14 AUGUST 1947—27 OCTOBER 1958)

SOON after the formation of Pakistan the leaders of the eastern wing began to realize that they were being cheated. The first blow was struck to their centuries-old language, Bengali. There were six major languages used in Pakistan : Bengali, Urdu, Punjabi, Pushto, Sindhi and Baluchi. Out of these six languages Bengali was used by 55.48 per cent of the whole population, whereas Urdu was used by only 3.65 per cent of the population. Being a language of the majority, Bengali deserved the status of the official language of Pakistan. Instead, Urdu was given this status. The Bengali cabinet ministers were forbidden to speak in their tongue in the parliament. This angered the Bengali population.

At Dacca, the Muslim students formed an Action Committee to ask for their rights. On 19 March 1948, Mr. Mohammad Ali Jinnah, first Governor-General of Pakistan, visited Dacca. In his public address he declared that Urdu will be the only national language of Pakistan. The audience left the place to indicate their protest. This was followed by demonstrations. All the schools and colleges were closed. Mr. Jinnah's portrait was removed from the classes. On 24 March 1948, Mr. Jinnah addressed a convocation of the Dacca University. Students demanded recognition of Bengali as one of the official languages. This upset the mood of the founder of a new nation. He branded these students as the enemies of Pakistan, and reiterated that Bengali could not be the language of the country. In September of the same year Jinnah died of cancer.

After Mr. Jinnah's death, Khwaja Nazimuddin was asked to be the Governor-General, but the real power remained with the Prime Minister Liaquat Ali, who appointed Ayub Khan as the Commander-in-Chief of the Pakistan army. Ayub Khan's promotion created unrest among many senior officers. On 16 October 1951, Liaquat Ali was killed by an Afghan. After his assassination Khwaja Nazimuddin became the Prime Minister, and the Finance Minister, Mr. Ghulam Mohammad, was nominated as the new Governor-General of Pakistan.

Khwaja Nazimuddin was educated at the Aligarh Muslim University. He was a staunch supporter of Urdu, though he was a Bengalee Muslim. The British Government knighted him for his services and loyalty to the Crown. As a Prime Minister, Khwaja Nazimuddin did nothing to reduce the agrarian problems, and never drew up any plans to ease the unemployment situation in East Pakistan. During his primeministership all the key positions in East Pakistan, such as those of secretaries, were given to Punjabis or to Urdu-speaking people. He was from an orthodox Muslim, feudal family of the Nowabs of Dacca, and as such was a blood-relation of other feudal lords. As an administrator he was very weak. Bengalees came to hate him.

During his office, agitation for the recognition of Bengali as one of the official languages did not stop. In February 1952, the Central Government attempted to introduce Persian script into the Bengali language. Peasants, students and workers arose as one to defend their mother tongue. On 20 February of the same year the Government banned processions and demonstrations. The Students

Federation broke the ban by organizing a big demonstration. The police were ordered to open fire on the demonstrators. As a result of the fusilade 26 students and peasants were killed and 400 were injured. This occasion is remembered by the people of Bangladesh as the Martyres Day. Due to increasing pressure, the Muslim League Government had to accept Bengali as one of the national languages. This partial success boosted the morale of Bengalees.

In September 1952, the Youth League and the Communist Party issued a call to all the political parties of the east to join together to ask for elections based on universal franchise. At this time people clamoured for self-rule; they began to demand autonomy for their province. The Muslim League Government, non-representative, knew that in any provincial or national election it would meet defeat. So, they kept procrastinating elections. In the spring of 1953, Dacca was torn with strikes, protests against discrimination, and demand for elections. In the autumn of that year resolutions were passed and mass meetings were held to press these demands with more vigour and enthusiasm. February the twenty-first was solemnized as the Martyres Day in commemoration of the Bengalees killed by the police in 1952. All the political parties got together to remember that day; the entire east was united. Citizens carried black banners.

In December 1953, all the political parties formed the United Front to oppose their autocratic rulers. Some of the political parties held diametrically opposed views. What united them was their sufferings at the hands of their common enemy, West Pakistan. The United Front proposed that the Central Government should be responsible only for defence, foreign affairs and currency, and in internal matters Provincial Governments should be autonomous.

The Muslim League Government had no concrete programme to counter the proposals of the United Front. It is said that, in religious garb, the Government sent people to the east to denounce the United Front and to convince the people that it was anti-Islamic, that it would weaken Pakistan, that it was financed by the Hindus of India, and that its leaders were selling East Pakistan to West Bengal, India. To divert their attention further, the Government launched propaganda to the effect that India was going to attack Pakistan. The principal leaders of the United Front were arrested; about 1,200 people were put behind the bars. The Government charged the leaders as agents of India. Some newspapers were banned. To weaken the movement, Hindu-Muslim enemity was also fomented. In fear, numerous Hindus immigrated to India between 1949 and 1953.

The Muslim League leaders presumed that these tactics would bring their government to power. The provincial election took place on 8 March 1954. In spite of these threats and arrests, the Muslim League suffered a crushing defeat. Many candidates of the Muslim League, including several members of the state cabinet, forfeited their deposits. Out of the total of 237 seats, the United Front won 223. The Muslim League got only 10 seats. Three went to independent candidates and one to a religious organization. The result of the election was a clear indication of the Bengalees' lack of confidence in their rulers, and of their determination to attain autonomy for their province.

A United Front Government, headed by Fazlul Haq as its chief minister, was formed on 3 April 1954. This coalition government began to work on its programme. Its victory affected the political climate of other parts of the country. The political parties of other provinces also demanded the dissolution of the non-representative Muslim League Government, and new democratic elections. Like

41

in the east, these parties tried to get together to form a coalition. A conference of all the political parties was summoned in the Northwest Frontier Province in April 1954. It was decided at this conference to establish a United Front along the lines of the one in the east. This was a sign of a forthcoming danger to the rulers. To weaken this move, they raised the slogan "Pakistan is in danger", and India was going to attack. Furthermore, they fomented bad blood between the East and West Pakistan, between Bengalees and non-Bengalees.

The deliberately instilled hostility between Bengalees and non-Bengalees resulted in their several clashes in East Pakistan. The worst of these took place at Adamjee Jute Mill in Narayanganj on 15 May 1954. Over 600 persons were killed and many hundreds were wounded. The Central Government asked the Coalition Government of the United Front to ban some political parties and put their leaders in jail. It refused to do so. However, it appointed a commission to investigate the riots that took place at Adamjee Jute Mill. It was discovered that the Muslim League Government was responsible for the riots. It became afraid of being exposed as the chief agent of the tragedy. Before the investigation could be completed, the Coalition Government was dissolved on 30 May 1954. The United Front Government was dismissed and the governor's rule was proclaimed. The defence secretary of the Central Government, Major General Iskander Mirza, was appointed as the Governor-General of East Pakistan. He was known for the suppression of Pakhtun's (people of the Northwest Frontier Province) national liberation movement. Major General Iskander Mirza imposed strict censorship on newspapers and banned all demonstrations and public meetings of any kind. Fazlul Haq, who presented the resolution for the formation of Pakistan at the All-India Muslim League conference in 1940 and who was

42

considered one of the founders of Pakistan, was declared a traitor and enemy of the country by the West Pakistani leaders. Fazlul Haq was put under the house arrest. Many cabinet ministers were imprisoned. The Governor of East Pakistan, Choudhary Khaliquzzaman, a Bengalee, was removed from his position.

During the first week of the Governor's Rule, 659 active members of the United Front were put behind the bars. Within a few weeks this number rose to about a thousand. The offices of the United Front were locked and their literature seized. The main charge against the United Front Government was that they wanted to establish an independent state, Bangladesh, whereas its leaders openly and repeatedly said that they simply wanted the provincial autonomy that was within the framework of the policy on which Pakistan was founded.

In spite of the strong repressive measures of the Government the spirit of the Bengalees could not be killed. Every harsh step of the rulers made Bengalees stronger, more adamant, in their demand for their rights. The situation deteriorated day by day. On 7 October 1958, Iskander Mirza, the president of Pakistan, imposed Martial Law throughout the country. General Ayub Khan, the supreme commander of the armed forces, was appointed as the Chief Martial Law Administrator. General Ayub Khan was himself looking for an opportunity to become the dictator of the country. On 27 October 1958, he forced the president, Iskander Mirza, to quit his office and leave Pakistan. He went to live in England, and General Ayub Khan took over the reign of Pakistan.

8—FIELD-MARSHAL AYUB KHAN'S RULE

(28 OCTOBER 1958—24 MARCH 1969)

ON 7 October 1958, a state of emergency was declared across Pakistan by the President Iskander Mirza. Ayub Khan at that time was the commander-in-chief of the land forces. He compelled Iskander Mirza to quit his office, and on 27 October Iskander Mirza handed over his powers to Field-Marshal Mohammad Ayub Khan.

Ayub Khan introduced a strict censorship over the press, prohibited the gatherings of more than five persons at any public place, and dissolved the Constitutional Assembly. He banned all the political parties, and arrested many writers and political leaders. He merged all the provinces of West Pakistan into one unit, dividing Pakistan into three zones: west, east and Karachi. Each of these zones was administered by a military officer. Ayub Khan became the president of Pakistan; the commanders of the airforce and of the navy became his deputies. A number of senior Bengalee officers were taken into custody. Major General Umrao Khan was appointed as the Martial Law Administrator for East Pakistan. Later on, he was offered the position of the Governor, but the judges of the High Court refused to administer the oath of loyalty to him. The Bar Association of Dacca passed a resolution to denounce Ayub Khan's repressive measures.

In spite of all his efforts Ayub Khan failed to stifle the voice of the people. Students in Dacca, Chittagong, Bogra,

Rajshai and at many other places demonstrated against the military regime. They demanded restoration of democracy and release of the political leaders. In fear of the growing discontentment, Ayub Khan gave to his country a constitution in 1962. After four years he abolished Martial Law, and gave to Pakistan a constitution which backed one-man's rule, that of Ayub Khan, for a further seven years with the support of the miltary. Bengalis rejected this constitution. Thousands of students at Dacca, Narayanganj, Comilla, Noakhli, Barisal, Kushtia, Chittagong, Sylhet, Mymensingh and Jessore organized violent demonstrations against the military dictatorship. They tore Ayub Khan's pictures. At Dacca they set a bus to fire. The president tried to divert the attention of the people with imaginary fears of attack by India and Afghanistan.

There was upsurge of anger and discontentment throughout the east. People demanded democracy. The increasing amount of unrest among the students was caused by two additional factors : The Central Government had decided to lengthen the duration of the B.A. degree course by one year, and restrictions were imposed on the students' participation in politics. As a result of the impositions, a number of students of the Dacca University were arrested and their degrees were rescinded. On 12 September 1962, students at Dacca organized a massive procession against the new controls; on 17 September they called for a general strike and protest meetings. The military were called in to disperse the demonstrators. Two persons were killed and about two hundred were wounded by the bullets fired by the soldiers. Ayub Khan dismissed the Vice-Chancellor of Dacca University contending that he could not curb the students' activities on and off the campus.

To make his position strong, Ayub Khan formed a political party named The Convention Muslim League. He provided many fascilities and benefits to those who joined his party. He got himself elected as its president. To win the sympathy of the Bengalee Muslims, he visited the cyclone-devastated areas and donated money to those who suffered. At the same time he disunited the citizens by creating a rift between Bengalees and non-Bengalees on the one hand, and Muslims and non-Muslims on the other. He prosecuted this plan through hired agents.

On 9 March 1964, Sheikh Mujibur Rahman, called Mujib by his associates, renewed the Awami League. To weaken this movement for democracy, Ayub Khan, on 1 July 1964, pressed the educational institutions to prohibit their teachers from participating in politics. On 24 September, the same year, there was a huge strike to force the government to release the political leaders. The strike met with a complete success. The government agreed to set the political prisoners free, although in Chittagong, police were ordered to open fire on the demonstrators—more than one hundred persons were killed. Sheikh Mujibur Rahman met President Ayub Khan to appeal to him to grant regional autonomy to East Pakistan, and to make it self-sufficient in defence. The demand for self-sufficiency in defence was a challenge to Ayub Khan. While Mujib was returning to Dacca via Jessore, he was arrested for a speech he had made. He was soon bailed out. An hour later, when he reached home, he was again arrested for another speech he had made at Sylhet. The next day he was freed on bail, but again he was arrested on a warrant from Mymensingh on the same grounds. The following day he was bailed out. In the second week of May he addressed a crowd at Narayanganj, and that very night he was imprisoned. His imprisonment was followed by the arrest of a number of leaders and members of the Awami League.

Around that time money was lavishly spent to develop the western wing at the expense of the eastern wing. Huge sums were being expended on Islamabad to convert that rugged land into a new capital for the country. To divert the attention of the Bengalees, Ayub Khan and his collaborators raised the problem of Kashmire, and carried out, with more vigour, propaganda against India. In September 1965 the war with India came. The eastern wing never favoured that war. As a matter of fact, it was never interested in the Kashmire issue. The eastern wing urged healthy, neighbourly relations with India, and resumption of trade which they thought would bring prosperity to the region. After the war, East Pakistan was compelled to bear the main burden of cost of that fruitless and unwanted war.

The Awami League once again called for a general strike on 7 June 1966 to bring pressure on the government to release the political prisoners. Eleven persons were killed at various places by the firing of the police on demonstrators, 800 workers were arrested.

Sheikh Mujibur Rahman was set free on 18 January 1968. The soldiers arrested him again at the gate of the prison. He was arrested on the charge that he attempted to topple the government with the aid of Indian money and her army; this is recorded as the Agartala Conspiracy Case. Mujib's arrest with other leaders led to violent demonstrations. All the political parties of the east joined together to fight for the restoration of democracy. President Ayub Khan rushed to Dacca, where he was greeted with black flags. The situation worsened when the news appeared in the Indian and some foreign papers that Ayub Khan's son and his son's father-in-law became millionaires in a few years through unfair profits from their industries. People began to denounce the president for his favouritism. It was also said that Ayub Khan had bought a farm in Sardinia, Italy, for his rainy days, and that he had a large bank balance in Geneva. It was also reported

47

in some newspapers that Ayub's daughter, Nasim, married in the Swat Royal Family, was involved in smuggling opium into Afghanistan. In fact, some files disclosed that Ayub himself was a partner of the great smuggler, Kasim Bhatti.

In September 1968, President Ayub Khan again visited East Pakistan. He tried to convince the Bengalees that democracy was not suited to Pakistan. The people greeted him with demonstrations and black flags. At that time the president faced a fierce apposition even in West Pakistan. There were public meetings against him across the country. In Dacca, 1,200 women broke the ban by demonstrating. Bengalees burnt the pro-Ayub newspapers, damaged government properties, and set buses on fire.

On 15 February 1969, a Bengalee soldier, Sergeant Zahural Haq, arrested in connection with Agartala Conspiracy Case, was killed in prison. The news spread like wild fire. Maulana Bhashani gave a fiery speech to a huge gathering. The crowd went mad and attacked pro-government elements. On 18 February, a professor of Rajshahi University was killed by soldiers during a demonstration. The incident infuriated the students and the workers alike. They defied curfew orders and went out of control. It was open rebellion. The masses, without arms and ammunition, challenged the military and tried to kill everyone whom they thought was pro-Ayub or supported his government. Human blood began to flow everywhere. It was a mass revolt without any planning or guidance. The administration was paralyzed. President Ayub Khan called the three commanders-in-chief of the armed forces, and asked for their assistance to control the situation. Agha Mohammad Yahya Khan, the commander-in-chief of land forces, did not agree. He advised Ayub Khan to hand over his office to the military.

President Mohammad Ayub Khan, still determined to

Plate 5—Body of one Zahiruddin, victim of Pakistan shelling in a school compound.

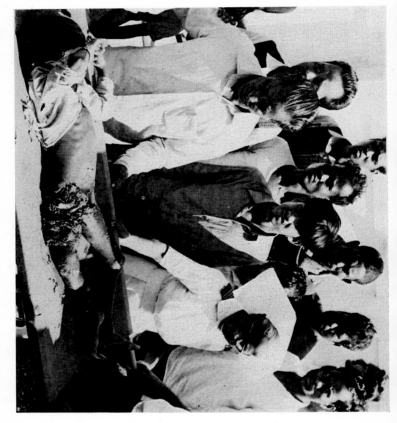

Plate 6—A child victim of Pakistan shelling on a stretcher.

cling to his position, broadcast assurances to the Bengalees that the constitution would be amended and that they would be given a larger share in running the government. The Bengalees turned a deaf ear. The demonstrations, the killing, the destruction of the government property continued. To calm the masses, Ayub Khan withdrew the Agartala Conspiracy Case and released the political prisoners, unconditionally. In spite of these measures the situation deteriorated. On 24 March 1969, President Ayub Khan, in a personal letter to Yahya Khan, wrote :

"It is with profound regret that I have come to the conclusion that all Civil Administration and Constitutional Authority in the country has become ineffective . . . I am left with no option but to step aside and I leave it to the Defence Forces of Pakistan, which today represent the only effective and legal instrument, to take over full control of the affairs of this country."

The letter, later on, was published in Pakistani newspapers. The next day he quit his office at the age of 61. He left for Swat, a small township 30 miles to the north of Rawalpindi, where two of his daughters were married into the Swat Royal Family. Sometime later, he left Swat to live in England.

4

9—GENERAL YAHYA KHAN'S RULE

(25 MARCH 1969—25 MARCH 1971)

GENERAL YAHYA KHAN assumed the reigns of Pakistan on 25 March 1969. The same day he declared Martial Law across the country. The next day he addressed the citizens on radio. He said : "by now you must also have read his (Ayub Khan's) letter of 24 March which is addressed to me and has been published in the press. . . . My sole aim in imposing Martial Law is to protect life, liberty and property of the people and put the administration back on the rails. . . . I wish to make it absolutely clear to you that I have no ambition other than the creation of conditions conducive to the establishment of a constitutional government . . . elected freely and impartially on the basis of adult franchise."

To make his position safe and strong, he dismissed many military and civilian officers, who were considered pro-Ayub Khan. Air Marshal Nur Khan was asked to resign; he was appointed the Governor of West Pakistan. Navy Chief S. M. Ahson, a senior Bengalee officer was also asked to resign to be the Governor of East Pakistan. In the month of August, he appointed his Council of Ministers; only those persons were taken on whom he could depend and rely. He banned the publication of some of the newspapers.

On 28 November 1969, he once again addressed his countrymen on radio. He promised them to hold a general election on 5 October 1970, and to convene the National Assembly to frame Pakistan's new constitution within 120 days. He added that if the National Assembly failed to accomplish its task within the period, it would stand dissolved. In that case, another National Assembly would be elected to do the work.

On 1 January 1970, Yahya Khan lifted the ban from the political parties. On the 30th of March, he issued the Legal Framework Order to guide the framers of the new constitution. The following are the salient points embodied in the Order :

1. Firm adherence to Islamic values.

2. Nothing should be done which could injure the unity and territorial integrity of Pakistan.

3. Maximum autonomy for the provinces as units of a Federal Unit.

4. The Federal Government shall have adequate powers to discharge legislative, administrative and financial functions, to discharge its responsibilities in relation to internal and international affairs, and to preserve the independence and territorial integrity of the country.

5. Complete regard for the defence needs of the country.

It was also stated in the Order that the constitution must be approved by the president (Yahya Khan) before it comes into force. If the president withholds his approval, the National Assembly shall stand dissolved. Any ambiguity in the Order shall be interpreted only by the president.

The people of East Pakistan did not like the Order, because Yahya Khan kept enormous powers in his hands, and assigned the Central Government absolute authority over the financial matters. They exhibited their displeasure through demonstrations. In August, General Yahya Khan postponed the general election from October to

December. The citizens were told that October, being a rainy month, was bad for voters. It was simply a pretext, as it is said, to give enough time to West Pakistani politicians to foment communal feelings among the easterners to divide their votes. Mujib and other leaders saw through Yahya Khan's plan. Bengalees began to fret and fume. In November, there were rumours that elections would be deferred indefinitely. Mujib is said to have told some foreign press correspondents that if elections are further delayed, he would demand complete separation for his region. Maulana Bhashani had already lost his faith in elections and in General Yahya Khan. He, therefore, withdrew his candidates from the contest.

On 13 November 1970, a severe cyclone hit East Pakistan. About a million persons died. Crops and houses were completely destroyed in certain parts where tidal waves went as high as 15 feet. The dead bodies of human beings and of animals were littered around. The B.B.C. disclosed that meteorological authorities in Pakistan entirely ignored the warning of the American weather satellite about the impending cyclone in the Bay of Bengal. The American weather satellite took pictures of a gathering violent hurricane on the 6th of November. The next day a warning was passed on to Pakistan meteorological authorities. It was later revealed that the warning was conveyed every day until the 12th of November, but the Pakistan Government did nothing to inform its people of the forthcoming disaster. Even after the 8 days of the cyclone, Pakistani rulers did not move to help the victims. It is ironic that the first persons who visited the affected areas were foreigners, and the first assistance ever to reach the victims was from overseas. Relief from Great Britain was the first to reach there.

Fifty-two advocates of the Dacca High Court demanded a judicial enquiry; they were convinced that the

Government's negligence and indifference was responsible for the tragedy. In London, East Pakistani students demonstrated in front of the Pakistan High Commissioner's office. The leaders of West Pakistan did not express their sympathy for the sufferers. Wali Khan, a leader of the Pakhtuns who also demanded autonomy for the North-west Frontier Province, was the only political leader from the west to visit the cyclone-stricken areas. The Government of India offered one crore rupees for the relief of the destitudes, but the West Pakistani leaders pressed Yahya Khan not to accept the offer from enemies. Instead of helping the victims, the newspapers and rulers indulged in anti-India propaganda. They attempted to frighten the citizens through fabrications such as India is massing her troops along the Pakistan's border to launch a sudden attack.

Bengalees were never led astray by the false propaganda, nor did the natural disaster discourage them. Day by day, they prepared themselves with more might and confidence to go to the first national poll to be held on 7 December 1970. The Awami League entered the campaign on the strength of its six points mentioned below :

1. The constitution shall provide for a federation of Pakistan in the true sense on the basis of the Lahore Resolution and for a parliamentary form of government based on the supremacy of a duly elected legislature by universal adult franchise.

2. The Federal Government shall deal with only two subjects : defence and foreign affairs—all the residuary subjects shall be vested in the federating states.

3. There shall be either two separate but freely convertible currencies for the two wings or one currency with two separate reserve banks to prevent inter-wing flight of capital.

4. The power to levy taxes and to receive revenue

53

shall be vested in the federation units. The Federal Government shall receive a fixed share to meet its financial obligations.

5. Foreign Trade : five steps shall be taken :

(1) There shall be two separate accounts for the earnings of foreign exchange.

(2) The earning of East Pakistan shall be under the control of East Pakistan, and the same shall be for the West Pakistan.

(3) Foreign exchange requirements of the federal government shall be met by both the wings either equally or in a ratio to be fixed.

(4) Indigenous products shall move free of duty within the wings.

(5) The constitution shall empower the unit governments to establish trade relations, and set up trade missions with foreign countries.

6. A militia or para-military force shall be created in East Pakistan which at present has no defence of its own.

The Awami League contested the December 1970 national election, first election since the formation of Pakistan in 1947, on the strength of its six-point manifesto mentioned above. Its popularity among the masses of the east can be gauged from the fact that it won 167 seats out of the total 169 allotted to East Pakistan in the National Assembly. The Awami League constituted an absolute majority in the chamber of 313 seats. There is no doubt that the representatives of the political parties of the minorities such as Scheduled Caste Federation and the National Congress would have backed the Awami League in the National Assembly. The policy of these political parties of the minorities falls along the lines of the Awami League. In the west wing, the Pakistan People's Party, headed by Mr. Z. A. Bhutto, secured 80 seats. It proved strong in the provinces of Sind and Punjab.

The National Assembly was scheduled to meet on 15 February 1971, to draft Pakistan's constitution in 120 days. On Mr. Bhutto's advice, General Yahya Khan deferred the Assembly's first meeting to 3rd March. The postponement of the Assembly without any apparent reason angered Bengalees. In any case, The Awami League prepared the outlines of the constitution, based on its six-point election manifesto. General Yahya Khan asked the Awami League's leaders to discuss the outlines of the constitution, with leaders of the political parties of West Pakistan, before the commencement of the National Assembly. As a result, the first meeting between Yayha and Mujib took place in Dacca in mid-January. Everything looked fine and satisfactory. The General asked Mujib to come to some understanding also with Mr. Bhutto concerning the constitution.

A number of meetings were held in Dacca between Mr. Bhutto and Mujib along with their associates. The discussion pivoted around the forthcoming constitution. During the private sessions, the members of the Pakistan People's Party did not indicate that any deadlock was reached. Rather, they told Mujib and his aides that they would talk further in the National Assembly. When Mr. Bhutto went back home, he announced his decision to boycott the National Assembly. In a press conference held at Peshawar (West Pakistan) on 15 February 1971, he urged others to do the same. Mr. Bhutto's main objections were against the six-point programme of the Awami League. Mr. Bhutto proposed that the Central Government should retain the control of trade and foreign aid; the Awami League's representatives refused to compromise on this point in the light of their bitter past experiences. During the election campaign, Yahya Khan and Mr. Z. A. Bhutto did not find any objection in the six points. They began to see defects in Awami League's election manifesto after

55

the party carried a landslide victory.

Mr. Bhutto's advice was not accepted by many elected members. Some of the members of his own political party had booked their seats in aeroplanes to attend the first National Assembly's meeting to be held at Dacca on 3rd March. The National Awami League, which dominated Baluchistan and the Northwest Frontier's Provincial Assembly, was fully committed to the six points. However, General Yahya Khan postponed the National Assembly indefinitely on the grounds that the political leaders lack unanimity of opinion on the constitution. The announcement was broadcasted on 1 March.

The Bengalees again arose to protest against Yahya Khan's decision. On 3 March 1971, Mujib asked his compatriots to launch a non-violent non-cooperative movement against the military regime. Demonstrations were held across East Pakistan. The military was called in to open fire on the protesters. About 350 persons were killed and 1,000 injured. The Dacca correspondent of the *London Observer* reported 2,000 killed by the armed forces. The non-cooperation was thorough and complete from 1 March to 25 March. The judges refused to administer the oath of allegiance to the Martial Law Administrator Tikka Khan. The police refused to obey the Government. The civilians remained absent from their offices. The shopkeepers refused to supply food to the army. During this period the workers of the Awami League carried on the work of administration. It is said that in comparison with the normal times the law and order was better maintained by the citizens.

Alarmed by the deteriorating situation, Yahya Khan, in his speech on the air on 6 March, promised to convene the National Assembly on 25 March. This time Mujib, in his speech made at Race Course, Dacca, on 7 March, asked that four conditions be met before he would form a government. The conditions were as follows:

1. Immediate end of Martial Law.

2. The soldiers must return to their barracks.

3. A public enquiry into the killings of the citizens by the armed forces.

4. Immediate transfer of power to the people's representatives.

Mujib addressed a crowd of a million people who expected from him a call for complete independence. He disappointed the multitude because he still favoured the idea of autonomy and of a united Pakistan. He, however, asked the citizens not to give revenue to the Government, and he asked the banks not to transfer money to West Pakistan. Consequently, the newspapers defied censorship to advise people how to achieve a successful non-cooperation with the Government. Telephone, telegraph and postal links were cut off between the wings. On the 15th of March Mujib took over the administration of the province.

The same day, 15th of March, Yayha Khan hastened to Dacca to negotiate with Mujib. The Awami League was in full control of East Pakistan. In the initial stages the talks were held mainly between Yahya and Mujib. Later on, Mr. Bhutto and his associates, and Mujib's helpers were asked to join them. On the 16th of March Yahya Khan is reported to have told Mujib during their talks that he was sorry for what had happened and he expressed his sincere desire for a political solution. It has been pointed out that during the talks Yahya Khan never indicated his disapproval of any of Mujib's demand. While the talks for reconciliation were on, the military shot 30 demonstrators at Joydevpur on the 19th of March. Meanwhile Yahya Khan accelerated his military build up in the east. Armed forces were brought in via Cylone, in civilian dress, on the commercial flights. The airport of Dacca was kept under strict control. Tanks from the border areas were brought in. On the 24th of March, orders were issued to unload the ship, Swat, which was full of ammunition, anchored at the port of Chittagong. It brought thousands of Bengalees to protest in the streets of Chittagong to prevent its unloading. The military opened fire. Brigadier Mazumdar, a Bengalee officer who commanded the garrison, was removed from his position and replaced by a West Pakistani.

On the 25th of March, Yahya Khan, Mr. Bhutto and other members of their group left for West Pakistan, without giving any message or warning to the Awami League leaders. As a matter of fact, Mujib and his aides were waiting for another talk on the 25th of March. They were simply surprised at their sudden departure. The same night at 11 p.m. the military with tanks, mortars, artillery, machine guns and rockets attacked the unarmed and sleeping civilians. That day changed the course of history. Bengalees, instead of asking for autonomy, began to fight for the complete independence of their region, now called Bangladesh.

General Yahya Khan was asked to resign on the 20th of December 1971, on the grounds of the loss of the eastern part. In Bangladesh the last day of his reign was the night, the 25th of March, when he ordered his troops to commit calculated genocide. From that hour Bengalees began to fight to drive the Pakistani army from their soil.

10—FIGHT FOR FREEDOM

MUJIB returned to his home called "Bang Bandhu Bhawan", after his talk with Yahya Khan on the 24th of March 1971. He appeared tired and depressed. The press correspondents asked him questions, but he remained silent. In a sad tone he began to mumble lines from a poem of Rabindranath Tagore. In crude English the lines could be translated as follows :

There is no fear
We will win surely
The prison's walls will break
Our chains will break
Freedom's door will certainly open.

While mumbling these lines, Mujib's face became radiant, perhaps, he began to realize that he had behind him a collective will of seventy-five million people. He suspected Yahya Khan's intentions when Yahya, Bhutto and company left for West Pakistan without leaving for Mujib any message. As a matter of fact, Mujib's party expected another talk on the 25th of March, the night Yahya Khan unleashed his terror. Mujib was asked to go into hiding that night. He refused to do so, because he knew that the military would raze the city of Dacca to the ground to find him. To avoid unnecessary killing, he remained at his home. Other leaders and students, who suspected Yahya's intentions, did not take precautions; they expected their arrest only.

59

The military launched its sudden attack on the 25th of March at 11 p.m. It used recoiless rifles, automatic weapons, bayonet, and tanks. Somewhere between 200 to 300 students of Dacca University were machine-gunned while asleep in their university hostel. Some newspapers put the figure from 350 to 400. Fourteen faculty members, some of them prominent scholars, were killed for their support of the Awami League. Seventy-five per cent of the university building was destroyed. Offices of two daily newspapers were set on fire. Shopping centres were wrecked; the shopkeepers were killed while asleep. Any moving figure within sight was shot. In 34 hours of wanton firing, about 10,000 persons were killed in Dacca alone. The air became fouled with the stench of dead bodies. For many days the city remained impassable without covering one's nose with a piece of cloth. Nearly half of the population of Dacca escaped to rural areas. The price of rice, the staple food of Bengalees, rose by 50 per cent. For many days offices remained closed. The city looked like a graveyard.

Though many women, children and old persons were killed, the main target of the military's wrath were students, leaders, teachers, engineers and other intellectuals, capable of providing the leadership and administration of the country. The people of this class, intelligensia, were considered dangerous to Pakistan's solidarity and unity. The fault of these people was their support of the ideology and philosophy of the Awami League, which won landslide victory in the December 1970 general election.

At the time of the attack, the 25th of March 1971, there were about 40 foreign correspondents in Dacca. They were asked to assemble at a hotel. After seizing the reports and films of the correspondents on the 26th of March, the military asked them to leave Pakistan. The reports of these correspondents published in the world press clearly demonstrated the truth that the people who were killed had no weapons, and there was no indication of any armed mutiny against the government. Some newspapers reported that the regional commander, Tikka Khan, was given only 48 hours to suppress the will of the people, who clamoured for the restoration of democracy. Yahya Khan probably feared intervention of foreign powers if the action was prolonged. Tikka Khan failed to accomplish his task within the time allotted. At Dacca, Bengalees were caught unaware; at other places, they prepared themselves to accept the challenge. Within 24 hours, Bengalees organized themselves into a liberation force called "Mukti Bahini".

To fight against 90,000 well-armed Pakistani troops, there were 9,000 members of the East Bengal Rifles, a border-patrol army that could frighten only petty smugglers. These were joined by 3,000 men from the East Bengal Regiment and 24,000 policemen. The people had only sharpened sticks, knives and axes. Numerous Bengalees rushed to India to beg arms. On the 26th of March the Mukti Bahini captured a small radio station to declare independent Bangladesh. On the night of the same day, Yahya Khan addressed the citizens on the radio. In his speech he blamed the Awami League for destroying the unity and integrity of Pakistan. He branded Mujib and his associates as enemies of Pakistan.

The military became desperate because of the growing resistance from the local people. It resorted to bombing villages. In Jessore, the Press Trust of India reported that thousands of Bengalees attacked the army to get hold of the airport. Bengalees had spears, clubs, axes and daggers; the Pakistani army killed 1,500 of them. In the district of Kushtia, north of Jessore, an Awami League leader told *The Times of London* correspondent that 300 soldiers were killing people in an effort to find some political leaders. Thirty thousand Bengalees surrounded the soldiers. When the army ran out of ammunition, the mob beat them to death.

It is estimated that 70,000 guerrillas fought for the liberation of Bangladesh. They controlled a large part of the countryside. The important cities were held by the Pakistani military. Within a few weeks, the Press Trust of India reported that guerrillas killed 3,000 West Pakistani soldiers. Bangladesh, a land with a confusing network of rivers and streams is an ideal place for guerrilla warfare.

On the 17th of April 1971, the elected representatives of the general assembly from the east got together near the Indian border to confirm Mujib's declaration of independence made on the 26th of March. Bangladesh declared itself a Sovereign Democratic Republic. Mujid was appointed president until the time its constitution was framed. It was decided that the assembly would act as a war-cabinet as long as Bangladesh was under Pakistani domination. The function, very simple, was attended by 10,000 freedom fighters, the members of the Assembly, some high officials of the provincial government and foreign correspondents. The proclamation was made by the Vice-President Syed Nazrul Islam. Portfolios were assigned as follows :

President : Sheikh Mujibur Rahman.

Vice-President : Syed Nazrul Islam.

Prime Minister : Tajuddin Ahmed.

Foreign Affairs, Law and Parliamentary Affairs : Moshtaque Ahmed.

Finance, Commerce and Industries : M. M. Mansoor Ali.

Interior, Supply and Rehabilitation : A. H. Kamruzzaman.

The Bangladesh war-cabinet moved its office temporarily to Calcutta, India. After a few months of warfare, the cabinet requested the Indian Government for military aid. The guerrillas had nothing with which to face Pakistani tanks, cannons and aeroplanes. In the month of December 1971, the Indian Government recognized Bangladesh. Bhuttan was the second country to give its recognition. After recognition, Indian troops entered Bangladesh to help the Mukti Bahini. After two weeks of fighting, all the Pakistani soldiers were arrested, and Bangladesh was freed from Pakistani rule.

11—STORIES OF ATROCITIES

DURING the nine month's civil war, many stories of atrocities committed by the Pakistani army have appeared in various newspapers across the world. These stories were sent to the newspapers by their own correspondents who visited the areas and interviewed the destitute. Some of the reports are given below.

The Hindustan Times, in its 30th March 1971 issue, describes how a woman and "her husband had run away from a train stopped by the army. Looking back they saw soldiers, perched on the compartments, shoot down hundreds of passengers. The rail tracks were strewn with hundreds of bodies of men, women and children." Alwyne Taylor, in his letter published in the *Daily Mail,* London, of 3rd April 1971, says that "Dacca is a death house. I saw so much that I won't be able to sleep for years." The Associated Press correspondent, Dennis Neeld and photographer Michael Laurent, made their way into Dacca from Calcutta (India), dodging West Pakistani Army. They went on foot and canoe. Their reports appeared in many newspapers of North America on 13th April 1971. They saw "a young girl cringed in a corner of the charred shell of her house. She clasped her baby brother in her arms and her eyes reflected fear . . . Neighbour said her parents died in the army attack." *Time* (Canada) of 3rd May, 1971, writes of "a young man whose house was

64

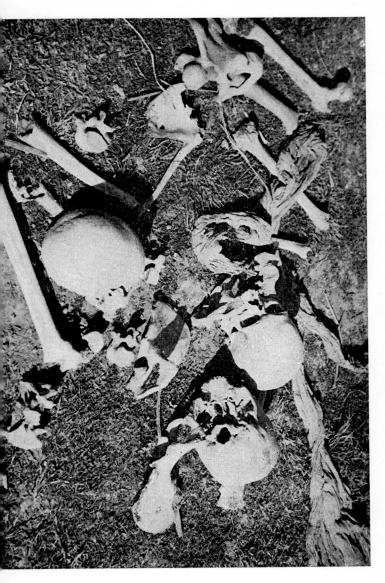

Plate 7—Evidence of genocide by Pakistan occupation troops. Some of the human skulls and bones exhumed at Khulna have been identified as those of young girls.

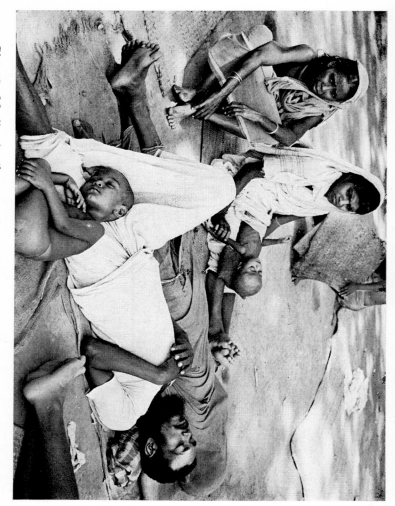

Plate 8—Muslim family at a refugee camp resting after a tiresome journey.

being searched begged the soldiers to do anything but to leave his 17-year-old sister alone; they spared him so he could watch them murder her with a bayonet."

Peter Hazelhurst, in his letter published in *Time* (Canada) on 23rd June 1971, describe tragedies of some of the Pakistani refugees recovering from bullet wounds. He met them at the hospitals near the border. Among many stories he writes, only three are included here. The first relates to Hasan Ali, a Muslim, whom he found lying at Casa Hospital near Bongaon. "The 25-year-old cultivator said that he and two friends were surrounded by 70 soldiers while working in their fields near Jessore in April. 'They wanted to know whether we were Hindus or Muslims. But they refused to believe we were Muslims. They started to shoot and I fainted.' " Peter Hazelhurst writes about Nethai Padanag, a young Hindu teacher who worked in a village of Mirzapur, in Jessore district. The teacher "lost his right arm and the three fingers of his left hand when a grenade was thrown through the window of his house last month." Haripada Rai, was a cultivator at Chunkuri, a village in the district of Khulna. Mr. Rai "and about a hundred Hindus were lined up along the bank of the Chunkuri river last month and machine-gunned by Pakistani troops. Miraculously he was hit in the side of his neck and he survived."

Mr. Colin Smith, who visited Dacca and from there flew over villages in a helicopter, writes in the *Observer* of 30th June 1971 that "East Pakistan has become a dreadful gold rush of horror stories. Every Bengali and non-Bengali has his own tale to tell. In Dacca the Bengalis say the murder of the non-Bengalis happened only in Chittagong, and go on to tell you of their own suffering." According to the *Montreal Star* of 2nd July 1971, the four British parliamentarians who toured East Pakistan impartially were convinced that Pakistani military did commit genocide. The military "behaved in an utterly un-civilized manner which would be a disgrace to any country in the 1970s. . . . The delegation leader Arthur Bottomley, a former minister of overseas development, said he was sure the Pakistan Army had indulged in a campaign of mass destruction and killing in East Pakistan."

Mr. Murray Sayle, the *London Sunday Times* corres-pondent describes his experience in an article that ap-peared in the *Montreal Star* of 26th July 1971. Mr. Sayle went to one of the villages ruined by Pakistani mili-tary. The empty village had indications of its being a Hindu village. He wondered where the inhabitants had disappeared. "Then, timidly, a woman in a tattered sari, with three young children at her heels, came forward. She was a Muslim and a refugee herself. Her husband had been killed and she had run away and found this empty village, as I had, by accident. She had been living on some rice the Hindus left behind. But it was finished and she was at her wit's end to feed her children. She did not want to go to the authorities because she was afraid they would find out her husband was 'Joi' Bangla (victory to Bengal), the slogan of the banned and smashed Awami League."

Dan Coggin, in *Time* of 2nd August 1971, describes of the refugees he met at the refugee camps. He says that every refugee "has his own horror story of rape, murder or other atrocities committed by the Pakistani army in its effort to crush the Bengali independence movement. One couple tells how soldiers took their two grown sons out-side the house, bayoneted them in the stomach and refused to allow anyone to go near the bleeding boys, who died hours later. Another woman says that when the sol-diers came to her door, she hid her children in her bed; but seeing them beneath the blanket, the soldiers opened fire, killing two and wounding another. According to one

66

report from the Press Trust of India (P.T.I.), 50 refugees recently fled into a jute field near the Indian border when they heard a Pakistani army patrol approaching. 'Suddenly a six-month-old child in it's mother's lap started crying,' said the P.T.I. report. 'Failing to make the child silent and apprehending that the refugees might be attacked, the woman throttled the infant to death.' "

Mr. Hugh McCullum, editor of *Canadian Churchman,* writes in the *Observer* of October 1971 : "I went into Bangladesh illegally. Whole sections of towns and villages on the Khulna-Jessore road are wrecked. I didn't go to Dacca, but the World Bank, never known as a liberal, bleeding heart organization, says 'it looks like a nuclear attack hit the university.' The central bazaar of Jessore is a mass of twisted rubble."

Mr. Sanjib Sarcar, editor of *The Aloke-Sarani,* Calcutta, interviewed many victims of Pakistani soldiers' barbarity for his book *The Bleeding Humanity.* From the many stories he gives, two are mentioned here. A seventy-year-old man told him "while he was coming towards India with his two sons, the armymen chased them. They killed one of his sons on the spot. He himself was injured and was carried here by another son." Sanjib Sarcar describes the experience of a journalist who took shelter in an empty, dark room on 26th of March, to find a way to escape. The journalist told Mr. Sarcar :

"There was a small hole in the room. He managed to peep through this hole and see a part of the street. Dead bodies were scattered on the street, on the pavement, slumped in the rickshaws, in front of the shops, everywhere, a street bathed in blood ! The houses along the street were damaged by the bullets and machine-gun fire."

The next day in the morning he saw this scene, as he describes in his own words :

"Suddenly I heard a truck stopping nearby. There were

67

entreaties of women . . . in a moment, cold sweat ran all over my body. Dumfounded I looked at the truck. It was loaded with girls and women of various ages. All of them almost without any clothing. Fear and panic had overwhelmed them. The truck was standing in the corner of the broad road, near the house in which I had taken shelter. The women and the girls were crying, weeping, tears rolling from their eyes. The Armymen were laughing at the entreaties of their victims. The women would not get down from the truck. The Armymen forced them to get down. And I saw the greatest hateful scene of the century performed before my eyes."

"It was 10.15 a.m. They raped in broad daylight all the women, young and old. The scene lasted for about an hour. The women almost lost their consciousness; some of them were half-dead. After an interval of a few minutes, the rifles roared. It was the end."

In *The Testimony of Sixty,* published by Oxfam, Oxford, Senator Edward Kennedy writes of his experiences based on what he saw and heard at the refugee camps. He says that "it is difficult to erase from your mind the look on the face of a child paralysed from the waist down, never to walk again; or a child quivering in fear on a mat in a small tent still in shock from seeing his parents, his brothers and his sisters executed before his eyes; or the anxiety of a 10-year-old girl out foraging for something to cover the body of her baby brother who had died of cholera a few moments before our arrival. When I asked one refugee camp director what he would describe as his greatest need, his answer was 'a crematorium'. He was in charge of one of the largest refugee camps in the world. It was originally designed to provide low income and middle income housing, and has now become the home for 170,000 refugees."

According to the news that appeared in *Time,* 20th

December 1971, the people of Jhingergacha told the *Time's* correspondent that the Pakistani soldiers shot the ones who did not understand their language, Urdu. Mr. Anthony Mascarenhas, assistant editor of the *Morning News,* a daily from Karachi, left his home with his family to inform the world of the military's atrocities. His articles have appeared in many newspapers. In the *Montreal Star* of 15th June 1971, he writes of his experiences encountered while touring the eastern part of the country, along with the military. At Chandpur, the military spotted a young boy running towards his home at twilight of one evening. Major Rathore reached for his Chinese-made machine-gun.

"For God's sake don't shoot," I cried. "He's unarmed. He's only a villager."

"Rathore gave me a dirty look and fired a warning burst."

"As the man sank to a crouch in the bush carpet of green, two jawans were already on their way to drag him in."

"The thud of a rifle butt across the shoulders preceded the questioning."

"Who are you?"

"Mercy, Sahib! My name is Abdul Bari. I'm a tailor from the New Market in Dacca."

"Don't lie to me. You're a Hindu. Why were you running?"

"It's almost curfew time, Sahib, and I was going to my village."

"Tell me the truth. Why were you running?"'

"Before the man could answer he was quickly frisked for weapons by a jawan. The skinny body that was bared revealed the distinctive traces of circumcision, which is obligatory for Muslims."

"At least it could be plainly seen that Bari was not a

69

Hindu."

"The interrogation proceeded . . . Abdul Bari was clouted several times with the butt end of a rifle, then ominously pushed against a wall. Mercifully his screams brought a young head peeping from the shadows of a nearby hut. Bari shouted something in Bengali. The head vanished. Moments later a bearded old man came haltingly from the hut. Rathore pounced on him."

"Do you know this man?"

"Yes Sahib. He is Abdul Bari."

"Is he a fauji?"

"No Sahib, he is a tailor from Dacca."

"Tell me the truth."

"Khuda Kassam (God's oath), Sahib, he is a tailor."

The journalist told the major "for God's sake let him go. What more proof do you want of his innocence?" Due to the intercession from the journalist "Rathore ordered Bari to be released. By that time he was a crumpled, speechless heap of terror. But his life had been saved." Mr. Mascarenhas continues:

"For six days as I travelled with the officers of the 9th Division headquarters at Comilla I witnessed at close quarters the extent of the killing. I saw Hindus, hunted from village to village and door to door, shot off-hand after a cursory inspection showed they were uncircumcised. I have heard the screams of men bludgeoned to death in the compound of the Circuit House (civil administrative headquarters) in Comilla. I have seen truckloads of other human targets and those who had the humanity to try to help them hauled off 'for disposal' under the cover of darkness and curfew. I have witnessed the brutality of 'kill and burn mission' as the army units, after clearing out the rebels, pursued the programme in the towns and the villages. . . ."

"And in the officers' mess at night I have listened

incredulously as otherwise brave and honourable men proudly chewed over the day's kill."

"How many did you get?"

"The answers are stored in my memory."

"All this is done, as any West Pakistani officer will tell you, for the 'preservation of the unity, the integrity and the ideology of Pakistan."

Mahila Parishad, a women's association of Bangladesh, made a fervent appeal to the U.N. to set up a special committee to enquire into the atrocities committed by Pakistani army on women. Begum Malika, its general secretary wrote to most of the world's women associations to pay their sympathetic attention to sufferings of women in Bangladesh. She alleged in her letters that wherever Pakistani military had its camps, it had also women's prisons to satiate their lust. In one of these prisons, near Calcutta, more than 150 women were tortured to death. Those who became pregnant were given poison by their relations to keep the family's prestige. Many of the women went mad, contracting diseases. Thousands of women in Bangladesh either killed themselves or went insane during the nine-month's action period. *India News,* published from Ottawa, writes in its issue of 5th January 1972 that "The Indian troops, with the help of International Red Cross, have rescued 51 young girls from various secret places in Narayanganj and Dacca cantonment in the past few days. The girls, aged 14 to 30 years, were found in rooms locked from outside by Pakistani troops. They were reported to be starving for a number of days. The girls narrated harrowing tales of atrocities committed on them."

The Ottawa Journal, in an article by Martin Stuart-Fox, appeared on the 9th of February 1972, writes of the atrocities committed on women. He describes about a young widow, Zobeda Begum of 20 years who "saw soldiers kill her husband. The soldiers then took her from the

71

village to the Dacca camp, releasing her when she became ill after six days. She said she didn't resist the soldiers because she was in a state of shock. Some girls attempted suicide, using their long hair or saris (long draped gowns) to strangle themselves, according to stories told to Mrs. Hamed. To prevent this Pakistani soldiers sometimes shaved and stripped the women." Mrs. Sahera Hamed, an organizer of the Bangladesh women's Rehabilitation Centre, says that "school girls, as young as 11 or 12, had been taken by the soldiers while on their way home from school." She says that the number of women who suffered will come to "hundreds of thousands. The Christian Relief Missions suggest the round figure of 200,000 women."

According to *India News,* Ottawa, "All India Radio's special correspondent says that during his visit to Khulna, he found three dumps of skeletons and skulls in the compound of the radio station which was completely destroyed by Pakistani soldiers before they surrendered to Indian army. The local people said those were remains of unfortunate girls held inside the radio station building by Pakistan army officers. The correspondent says, when he visited the liberated towns and hamlets, he found bodies of girls brutally murdered inside some of the bunkers."

Newsweek, in its cover story of the 2nd of August 1971 issue, writes that the wounded West Pakistani soldiers needed blood. Army commanders forced Bengalees to lie down. "Needles were inserted in their veins and then slowly the blood was drained from their bodies until they died."

Around ten million Bengalees escaped to India to evade death, and about three million dollars were needed daily to feed them. The refugees, from every walk of life and religion, took shelter under roofs, tents, trees and in empty water pipes. The influx, the greatest the world has so far known, consisted of infants, children, old men and women, ill, hungry, exhausted, terrorized, wounded, orphans and so on. Though the world community extended its generosity to help the destitute, yet the main burden of feeding them fell on the shoulders of India, already a poor nation of 500 million people. To aggravate the plight, cholera broke out in some of the refugee camps; it took thousands of lives.

David Loshak, a prominent journalist, in his book *Pakistan Crisis,* calls the massacre "more methodical, planned, and ruthlessly executed than any in modern times since the Nazis". He further says that "whole areas of the town of Khulna were burned down in an operation officially described as 'slum clearance' : at times, the river was choked with corpses. Soldiers at Santihar destroyed almost the entire town and shot every Bengalees they could find, on sight. At refugee camps in India, there are Pakistani babies that have been bayoneted. At Kushtia, Punjabi soldiers raided the house of a businessman and killed all but one (left for dead) of a family of seven. At a village in the east of the province, soldiers murdered two children before their mother's eyes and then shot her as she held the baby. John Hastings, a Methodist missionary in Calcutta, says he has certain evidence that soldiers threw babies in the air and caught them on bayonets and killed girls by thrusting bayonets into their vaginas" (p. 115).

For months after its independence the stories of atrocities continued escaping the pens and mouths of visitors to Bangladesh. According to a report published on page four of the *Canadian India Times* of the 7th of December 1972, Lotta Hitschmanova, an internationally known woman for her humanitarian work, made these remarks at a gathering in Vancouver, Canada, on the 25th of November 1972 : "What I saw in Bangladesh recently was so shattering that I thought I would have a break down, the first time that I just couldn't take it." Showing the slides she said, "the butchering of the students, the intellectuals, the barbarious rape of very near every Bengali lady including the minors, the burning and looting of every house and the belongings by the West Pakistani soldiers, seemed unbelievable, but it is a fact. The tyrants and the troddens both were the followers of the same Prophet Mohammed."

12—INDIA'S ROLE

THERE is no doubt that creation of an independent Bangladesh was in India's interest for many reasons. India spent a huge amount to keep armed forces along the border of her hostile neighbours. Cordial and friendly relations with Bangladesh would go a long way to help her reduce her military expenditure and to concentrate fully on the western border. India also hoped for resumption of trade between both the countries for the sake of mutual benefit. The Pakistani rulers had created a problem for India by training and militarily equipping the Naga rebels of Assam, who claimed a portion of India in which to establish an independent Nagaland. They had their permanent sanctuaries in Pakistan. The Indian government hoped that Bangladesh government would cooperate with her to control activities of these rebels. Apart from these expectations, millions of Indians have religious, cultural and linguistic ties with the people of Bangladesh. The worst sufferers at the hands of Pakistanis was the Hindu community of Bangladesh. For months Mrs. Indira Gandhi was under constant pressure from the Indian masses to check the reign of terror unleased on the Bengalees. But she was very cautious to take any step which could be considered as intervention in the domestic matters of others.

A problem is domestic as long as it does not cross a country's geographical boundaries and become a menace to neighbours. Pakistan's calculated massacre of the Bengalees shook the econo-political structure of an adjacent nation. To evade death, ten million Bengalees fled to India. In keeping with her traditional hospitality India gave them food and shelter. A few years before this, she showed her hospitality to the Dalai Lama and his compatriots when Tibet was captured by the Red China. The Indian government found for them means of livelihood, though she had to incur the wrath of China, which resulted in its attack on India. This time India opened her doors to let in the destitute of Pakistan. It needed 3.3 million dollars a day to give them minimum care. When the Indo-Pakistan war broke out on the 3rd of December 1971, the international community had pledged only 200 million dollars for the relief of refugees; this was a meagre sum from India's point of view. Naturally an armed conflict with Pakistan to enable the refugees to go back was much a cheaper solution to the problem than to keep them indefinitely. The journalists, humanitarians and statesmen repeatedly warned the world against the inevitability of war between India and Pakistan. Based on a close study of the deteriorating situation some of them had even set the approximate dates of the anticipated war. In spite of their prognostics and pleas none could do anything to avert it.

India foresaw another problem which she would have to face. She feared that in a prolonged guerrilla warfare leadership might slip from Mujib's Awami League to the extreme radicals. A pro-Peking group was already engaged in destructive activities in the Bengal province of India, which is on the border of Bangladesh. A similar pro-Peking group, though with a different name, was active and had considerable strength in Bangladesh. In the absence of any natural barrier on the border, it was easy for the guerrillas to move to and fro, creating a serious threat to India's internal security. India sincerely desired to have the civil war in Pakistan ended at its early stage.

India waited for months for the international community to come up with any feasible solution. In the absence of any alternative, she took it upon herself to settle the matter by assisting the Bengalis in their cause. The United States and Red China strongly condemned India on the grounds that she intervened in Pakistan's domestic affairs. Any student of politics can tell that the United States did interfere on one pretext or the other in the domestic affairs of the Congo, South Africa, Southern Rhodesia, Cyprus and Vietnam. The article 20(3) of the Universal Declaration of Human Rights states that the "will of the people shall be the basis of the authority of government; this will shall be expressed in periodic and genuine elections which shall be by universal and equal suffrage and shall be held by secret votes or by equivalent free voting procedure." The Bengalees expressed their will in the December 1970 national elections, when the Awami League emerged as the strongest political party in the country. Being a supporter of democracy, the United States was expected to convince or compel Pakistani militarists to respect the wishes of the people. Also, China, as a supporter of the people's revolution, should have adopted the same policy. Instead, both the countries sided with Pakistani rulers, regarding genocide as internal matter of the country. The strange attitude of their key leaders could be understood in the light of Russia's role and its friendly ties with India. Both the countries sacrificed their ideologies for the sake of their self-interests. As far as U.N. is concerned, it restricted its operation to humanitarian work.

India's military operation cost her the loss of 73 tanks, 45 planes, and one warship. From her army, 2,307 were killed; 6,163 were wounded and 2,163 were missing.

Besides, numerous civilians were killed or suffered in one way or the other. Pakistan did not release a list of its losses, but according to an Indian announcement Pakistan lost 244 tanks, 94 combat planes, two submarines, 16 gunboats and 12 miscellaneous craft. The list of casualties should be longer than that of India.

Some Indians as well as others believe that one of the motives of India to enter into this expensive warfare was to weaken Pakistan militarily and to create permanent peace on the sub-continent. A coterie of Pakistani intellectuals hold that rivalry and jealousy among the military commanders proved fatal for the country. They were keenly interested in the politics to grasp the country's reins by ostracizing Yahya Khan from his power. For instance Air Marshal Rahim, a Bhutto man as subsequent events have proved it, did not give his expected help to the ground forces.

Whatever the reasons of Pakistan's total defeat could be, it is obvious that India had no expansionist's ambitions. India gave her official recognition to Bangladesh long before it was expected. This was done mainly to remove the doubts and suspicions of other nations that India wanted to occupy Bangladesh. By giving her recognition she enabled Bangladesh government to take the charge of whatever territory India would free from Pakistan.

13—EPILOGUE

THE RACE COURSE of Dacca is like an old woman who has seen many ups and downs in her children's life. This is the ground where gatherings of different political parties were held, and where Mr. Mohammad Ali Jinnah addressed the Bengalees for the first time after Pakistan's formation. On the 21st of March 1948 a crowd of more than a million Bengalees was gathered here to hear a lecture of Mr. Jinnah, the founder of Pakistan. Everyone was in high spirits, hoping for a bright future. The crowd was rending the sky with its slogan, long live Pakistan. Mr. Jinnah asked the Bengalees if they could afford to lose Pakistan through carelessness and negligence. The whole atmosphere was filled with the roars of never, never. Mr. Jinnah urged them to work for the unity and solidarity of Pakistan to make it stronger. He assured the Bengalees that they were a part of Pakistan and that he obtained it mainly with their support. At that time the majority of Bengalees were ready to do and die for Pakistan.

After 24 years there was again a crowd at the Race Course, but this time its motive was different. The whole of Dacca looked sad and desolate. Tall and magnificent buildings which once were the pride of Pakistan, appeared lonesome. Pakistan's flag was seen nowhere—the only flags which fluttered around were of Bangladesh and of India. The sound of firing was audible at short intervals. Towards the evening thousands of Bengalees with spears, axes and guns rushed to the Race Course to witness the ceremony of the Pakistani army's surrender. They were furious with the Pakistanis, and their every action reflected their deep-rooted contempt for them.

The causes of this tremendous change in the Bengalees' hearts have been discussed in the foregone chapters. It is understandable that if Pakistani rulers had accepted the majority's demand for restoration of democracy, Bangladesh even today would have been a component part of Pakistan. As far as the causes of bloodshed and defeat are concerned, many interesting factors were considered in the news media after the dust of the battle was settled. Most of them could be summed up under miscalculations of Yahya Khan. In the ninth chapter, entitled "Fight For Freedom," it has been brought to the reader's notice that the Awami League won a landslide victory in the December 1970 national elections. In a normal way, the leader of the Awami League should have formed his government. Instead, he was imprisoned, his party was banned, and his country was ravaged. Ten million Bengalees escaped to India. The question may arise why Yahya Khan allowed the Awami League to contest the election when he did not approve its policy and principles?

As a matter of fact, Yahya Khan was given to understand by the military intelligence that the Bengalees' demand for autonomy was the whim of a handful of leaders and that the masses did not favour this demand. Yahya Khan assumed that by threats and diplomatic devices he would be able to split further the already divided electorate. Hence the national assembly would be a mixture of representatives of various factions. He expected to win to his side some of the representatives, who would assist him to carry on his military administration in the garb of

80

Plate 9—Distraught old lady with injured hand.

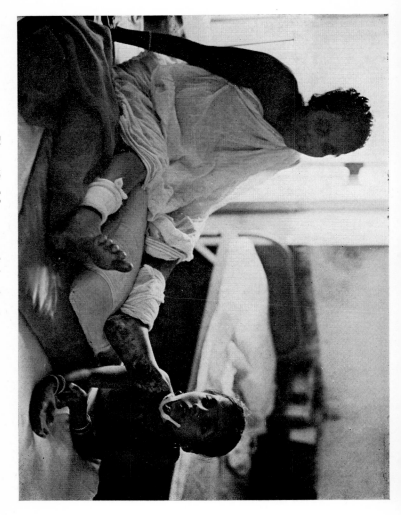

Plate 10—More wounded refugees at a camp.

democracy. But the result of election killed his aspirations. The Awami League emerged the strongest political party, which confirmed the fact that autonomy was the demand of the people.

Yahya Khan did not abandon his hope to drive Mujib according to his wishes. He thought of doing so by putting Mujib in a very difficult position, especially by disuniting the politicians. Therefore he gave full liberty to Mr. Zulfikar Ali Bhutto, Mujib's enemy, to make all sorts of provocative and irresponsible statements, though the country was under Martial Law. This freedom was denied to the leaders of the Awami League. Yahya Khan's chief objective was to play an arbitrator's role in order to exercise a decisive influence on the country's political life. Mujib, having the support of seventy-five million people, had enough self-confidence to deal with the military dictator. When Yahya Khan failed to use Mujib as a rubber stamp, he played his next trump—it was the postponement of the meeting of the national assembly. Mujib met this challenge by asking his followers for non-cooperation with the military regime. His call was respected by the judges of the High Court, peasants and factory workers alike. On every building, house, and factory the banner of Bangladesh began to be seen.

Yahya Khan faced the situation with might. He ordered the military to crush the non-cooperation movement within forty-eight hours, for he feared that a long military operation might invite intervention of some foreign powers. The military failed to achieve its goal. It confronted fierce opposition at every step. The clashes between soldiers and civilians lingered on for months, causing substantial losses on both the sides. Though the military let loose a campaign of genocide, the main victim of its wrath was the intelligensia. Yahya Khan prosecuted this campaign to annihilate intellectuals who could successfully shape Bangladesh's future. Through mass-murder, he thought he would reduce the population of the east, and this would minimize the strength of the Awami League. To get rid of the unwanted people and also to create economical as well as political headache for India, he forced ten million Bengalees to seek refuge there. Defeat and frustration once again dogged Yahya's footsteps. The ten million refugees helped India to win the favour of many countries. The parliamentarians and the correspondents of the world press interviewed the refugees. Their reports, published in the newspapers, revealed the barbarity committed by the Pakistani army. India received some financial assistance from other nations, along with their appreciation and good will, to look after the refugees. On the other hand, Pakistan was condemned and denigrated.

Due to his stubbornness, Yahya Khan was in no way willing to surrender before the democratic forces. He imagined that India would never dare to intervene in the so-called Pakistan's domestic affairs. He had full reliance on China's and the United States' promises for support. He built his military position stronger on the Kashmire border, thinking that after any armed conflict with India he would be in a better bargaining situation if he could snatch a considerable portion of Kashmire. It was another delusion of the military dictator. In the war, Pakistan lost its eastern province, and on the western front its losses were no less than incalculable. Its 95,000 soldiers were arrested. China and the United States did nothing, except to make occasional threats to India.

After the historical defeat, Yahya Khan stepped down to hand his power to Mr. Zulfikar Ali Bhutto. The new president put Yahya Khan under house arrest, and relaxed the restrictions which his predecessors had imposed on the press. In retrospect, citizens deliberated the causes of the defeat and the humiliation caused by it. According to the news published in local and foreign press, Yahya Khan's extraordinary interest in wine and women was the major cause of defeat. *Urdu Digest,* Lahore, Pakistan, disclosed some of Yahya Khan's incidents concerning them in an article appeared in January 1972 issue. The author says that the whole administration was victimized by these evils. Instead of thinking of the country's welfare, Yahya Khan and his associates were involved with wine and women. The country was at war and they were looking for new girls. The nation was governed by a few prostitutes, a fact which everyone knew in Pakistan. The promotions and transfers were determined by the employees' capacity to provide them. Money was lavishly spent to build the State Bank's guest house, which had a bedroom fully covered with mirrors. This room was used for the recreation of the senior officials. The article reveals that in Rawalpindi every child knew that once Yahya Khan went to an officer's house, where he spent two days and nights. He did not like to come back from that house. On the advice of his mistress Yahya Khan raised her husband to the rank of ambassador.

The article states that many officers offered their wives and daughters to their seniors to gain promotions. The ones who refrained from doing so, could achieve nothing. In the same article the author assumes the possibility of a conspiracy of some elements which wanted to weaken Pakistan to restore peace in the sub-continent. Whatever the reasons, it is obvious from Bangladesh's struggle that no power on earth can crush the will of a people who are bent upon achieving the status of self-determination.

PART II

BANGLADESH—BACKGROUNDS AND PERSONALITIES

_____

14—ANOTHER FIGHT

BANGLADESH had to prepare itself for another fierce fight after winning its freedom and that fight was against the problems created by the war. One of them was the rehabilitation of ten million refugees who sought shelter in India during those turbulent days. They, including millions of other Bengalees, had their cattle killed to feed the Pakistani army and their houses were destroyed and property looted. Bangladesh's infant government had neither money nor material nor transport facilities to help refugees make a fresh start in life. Some of the building materials, such as cement, had to be imported and the country was almost bankrupt and the transport system was badly shattered.

Riots, fear, war, and exodus of citizens left most of the land uncultivated. The plantations of Sylhet, which produced 68 million pounds of tea annually, were ruined. The country's main foreign exchange earnings come from the export of jute, but jute farming suffered during the war. The Pakistani army did not destroy many of the jute mills, because one-third of them were owned by non-Bengalees. But many months after the war, many factories could not be worked to their full capacities due to lack of skilled managers and administrators, who came largely from Pakistan. The work was slowed down also for want of material and capital to run the factories.

Bangladesh is a land of rivers and much of the transport depends on boats. Many of the ferries were wrecked or rendered unserviceable. Also many bridges were destroyed either by the Pakistani army or by the guerrillas to check movements of their enemies. The railways suffered the most because two of the largest bridges, Harding Bridge over the Ganges on the west border and the King George VI over the Meghna river on the east border, were blown. In all about 250 bridges were destroyed.

The retreating Pakistani army created threat and insecurity for the citizens by freeing every prisoner. Also the army removed all the radio sets from the police stations, razing some of the stations to the ground. Five thousand policemen were killed in the war. As a result, armed robberies became the order of the day after independence. The infant government had to recruit new men to train for police work. The government had to find radio sets and build police stations too. It was a real problem to recapture prisoners who had received arms from the Pakistani army.

The country was almost bankrupt when it was freed. Most of the banks were owned by Pakistanis. During the war, they transferred their capital to Pakistan. Even the mill-owners took their money and heavy equipment to their country.

According to the Bangladesh Government between three and four billion dollars were needed to raise the country to its pre-war economic level. To save money, the government froze salaries and even introduced cuts in the salaries of the senior employees. Side by side, the government nationalized jute plants, domestically owned banks, insurance companies, sugar mills and most of the shipping services.

The government gave first priority to agriculture. Consequently, the government introduced reforms and granted

85

loans to farmers for the purchase of pumps, fertilizers, pesticide, etc.

The Christian Organization for Relief and Rehabilitation, a Roman Catholic group, and about fifty experts from Japan helped villagers use power cultivators where bullocks were not obtainable. The United Nations, New Zealand and Russia sent their aircraft to make assistance quickly available to the people living in places inaccessable by roads. Some British specialists solved the problems concerning wrecked bridges. Soviet experts removed barriers caused by sunken vessels. But most of the assistance in the form of men and material came from India.

15—GEOGRAPHY AND CLIMATE

BANGLADESH is the 139th independent nation of the world, and in terms of population it ranks eighth among the world's 148 countries. It covers an area of about fifty-six thousand square miles. The total population is seventy-five million, and density of population is 3,000 persons per square mile. About 76 per cent of the population depend on agriculture for their livelihood. The country is surrounded on three sides by the Indian states of West Bengal, Meghalaya, Assam and Tripura. On the south it is bordered on the Bay of Bengal. It has common border with Burma towards the south-east. The closest countries to the north of Bangladesh are Nepal, Sikkim, Bhuttan and Tibet—Tibet is a part of Red China now.

Bangladesh lies between 20° 30′ and 26° 45′ North Latitude, and 88° and 92° 56′ East Longitude. The country's capital, Dacca, lies on the bank of the Burhiganga river which is a distributory of the Dhaleswari.

Except towards east and the south-east where the country has hills, most of the land is flat, even and alluvial and is intersected by numerous rivers and their tributaries. Many places, though 100 miles from the sea, are not more than 30 feet above sea level. A few feet rise in the sea water is enough to bring most of the land under water. All the rivers flow southwards, towards the Bay of Bengal. They join ultimately the Ganges. One of the perennial rivers is Jamuna which is fed by the Brahmaputra, the Meghna and the Ganges itself. Although rivers cause flood and waste in monsoons, they provide cheap means of transport and help in uniting different parts of Bangladesh.

In general terms, the climate of the country may be described as moderately warm and humid. The maximum temperature, except in two or three places, arises in April. Temperature in summer ranges from 91° to 96° F. Most of the country is situated to the north of the tropic of cancer, yet it is called a tropical country because its climate is warm. Winter lasts from the end of November to the middle of January. During these months the temperature ranges from 45 to 50 degrees.

Humidity is high throughout the year—it varies from 75 to 82 per cent. The months of June and July are very humid—84 to 90 per cent. June to September are the typical monsoon months. The average annual rainfall in many parts of the country is more than sixty inches. The northern and north-eastern portion of Sylhet district receives from 150 to 200 inches of rain. It does not rain much in winter.

Cyclones have been disastrous for the people of Bangladesh. Their effect is felt mostly in the southern part, like Chittagong, Noakhali and Barisal.

The famous cyclone named Bakarganj Cyclone, which occurred on the 31st of October 1876, attacked an area of 3,000 square miles in Chittagong, Noakhali and Bakarganj. It took the lives of 400,000 persons. The Chittagong Cyclone of the 31st of October 1897 killed about 175,000 people. The cyclone of the 1st of November 1912, known as Khulna-Faridpur Cyclone, and another on the 24th of September 1919, resulted in the death of 40,000 persons. In October 1960, two cyclones devastated the area in an interval of three weeks. The first cyclone hit the coast on the 10th of October, killing around 4,000 people. The tidal waves went as high as ten feet and were accompanied by a wind of 80 miles per hour. People had hardly recovered from the first cyclone when the second one attacked them after three weeks, on the 31st of October. The wind speed arose to 100 miles per hour. The cyclone caused a havoc at the Chittagong seaport. Many anchored ships broke away and were grounded. The cyclone took a heavy toll of lives, from 7,000 to 10,000.

Another devastating cyclone hit Barisal, Noakhali, Faridpur, Comilla and Dacca districts on the 11th and 12th of May 1965, and killed about 15,000 people. The wind speed ranged from 100 to 120 miles per hour. The cyclone, which surpassed all the former ones in its destruction, was the one which hit the country on the 13th of November 1970. About a million persons died. Crops and houses were completely destroyed and in certain parts tidal waves went as high as fifteen feet. According to an estimate 600,000 tons of rice was lost, and 367,000 homes were wrecked.

The cyclones normally hit in the night and remain in full fury till morning. They demolish houses, destroy crops, kill animals and uproot trees, and take human lives.

16—NATURAL RESOURCES

BANGLADESH'S most important natural resource is its water. Its mighty rivers are fed with the snow and water that fall on the eastern part of the Himalayas. These rivers, with a number of their branches and adjuncts which intersect Bangladesh in various directions, provide the country with a cheap and easy system of navigation and employment to thousands of boatmen. In a land of rivers, it is very expensive to expand its rails and roads. That is why the Pakistani rulers did not bother to develop Bangladesh's transport system.

Transportation, which is essential for the development of a country's economy, is carried on in Bangladesh mostly by waterways. Many of the country's large and deep rivers are navigable all the year round for all sorts of vessels. Other rivers can be used only in certain seasons or by small boats all the time.

In comparison with rail and road transports, the waterways are slower and become much slower in dense fogs. But the usefulness of rivers is enhanced in monsoons and during floods, when other means of transport are rendered unusable.

Rivers abound in fish and crocodiles. All of them are useful to earn foreign exchange. Fish is the staple food of Bengalees, and it is also exported. The Bay of Bengal possesses immense potential for the manufacturers of various oils and fish products.

90

Forests play an important part in Bangladesh's economy. The total area covered by them is 8,558 square miles, out of which 4,600 square miles come under Reserved Forests. Most of the forests are in the south and south-east of the country, and they range from typical evergreen to the cane, bamboo and green forests of the low-lying plains. The forests provide different kinds of wood. Some kinds of timber are used for match-sticks, for match-boxes, posts, railway sleepers, ships, electric poles, boats, etc. The bark of certain trees is used for tanning purposes. The forests provide also natural honey and bees wax, which are normally exported. The skin of some reptiles, such as lizards, are also used to earn foreign exchange. The bamboos are useful for house construction, to make handles of umbrellas, and to make papers. The paper mills of Chandraghona, near Kapti, and the news-print factory of Khulna rely on these forests for their raw material.

Some primitive tribes still dwell in some of the teak forests. Animals like elephants, Bengal tigers, panthers and leopards infest some of the tangled jungles, many of which are in the Chittagong Hill Tracts.

The Pakistan Petroleum Company found traces of natural gas about fifteen miles to the east of Sylhet, in 1955. The natural gas was discovered about 1,100 feet below the surface. A spark from the nearby kitchen struck the deposit and burnt all the gas. This negligence caused some damage to Bangladesh's future development. About two miles from there, the company dug another well to trace the availability of the gas. It was discovered at a depth of 9,245 feet, but its pressure was so high that it went almost out of control. The operation was ceased and the well was closed.

Later some more wells were successfully drilled. A fertilizer factory was established at Fenchuganj. This factory generates electricity, and manufactures synthetic fertilizer, known as Urea. In some of the factories gas has completely taken the place of imported coal.

The natural gas was also discovered at a place, fifty miles from Dacca, and in Comilla district. It is estimated that the total reserve of natural gas in Bangladesh is four million million cubic feet. This gas is 95 per cent methane. Plans exist for an extensive petro-chemical industry based on gas. Some explorations were made for oil, so far with discouraging results.

For the industrial development of Bangladesh, availability of cheap fuel is indispensable. So far, coal is the main source of heat in the country and nearly all of it is imported. Coal has been discovered in Sylhet and Comilla, but it is not of fuel grade.

17—AGRICULTURE

BANGLADESH is, primarily, an agricultural country. Sixty-four per cent of its total area is under cultivation and about 82 per cent of its population depends on agriculture for its livelihood. Agriculture provides food for the people and raw material for the country's factories. Such a mainstay of the nation is largely dependent on the unpredictable rainfall—slightly late, early, heavy or little rainfall proves harmful for the crops. Floods often destroy a large portion of crop every year. At certain places, water is stored in wells and tanks during monsoons to be used for irrigation during the dry season.

Agriculture is not mechanized; it is still carried on by primitive methods, bullocks and two sticks with a plough. Large landholdings are rare. The average size of a landholding is 3.5 acres. Forty-two per cent of the land is in the hands of the cultivators who have less than five acres. A programme for pumping water from rivers was initiated in 1968, but not on a massive scale. Sheikh Mujibur Rahman's government has given first priority to agriculture and gives loans to cultivators to buy better seeds and to use improved methods for cultivation.

Bangladesh does not produce enough food for its people, in spite of the fact that a large portion of the country's land is under cultivation and a majority of the population is employed in agriculture. A few decades ago, the cultivators raised their own food on their plots of land.

93

If a cultivator's land was not enough he would work as a hired labourer on another cultivator's land and receive a part of their crop as his wages. In his book published in 1916, J. C. Jack writes: "The life of the cultivator in Eastern Bengal (now Bangladesh) is in many ways a very happy life. Nature is bountiful to him, the soil of his little farm yields in such abundance that he is able to meet all his desires without excessive work. He can produce the food of his own family and sufficient to purchase everything else which he requires from a few acres of land that he can cultivate unaided without overwork. The whole of his labour is over in three months if he grows a rice crop only."[5]

The prosperity of which J. C. Jack speaks in 1916, gradually began to disappear. The life of cultivators grew miserable as the food became scarce. There could be many reasons for this change. One of the reasons is lack of mechanized agriculture to meet the need of rapidly growing population. Another reason could be cultivators' interest in jute. Since the introduction of jute and its increasing demand, the cultivators began to grow more jute. Most of the land in Bangladesh is very suitable for rice, but the cultivators prefer to raise jute because it brings them more profit. As a result, Bangladesh became an importer of food.

Bangladesh is the largest producer of jute in the world. Other countries which produce jute are India, Formosa, Nepal, Thailand, Iran, Egypt, Sudan, Turkey, West Africa, Java, Brazil and Mexico. Jute is used to make a number of articles. Its yarn is mixed with cotton, wool, silk, flax and many other fibres to produce curtains, rugs, carpets, buckram, cable, cords and a host of other things. Its importance has slightly declined since the discovery of synthetic fibres. The U.S.A., once a major buyer of jute, now relies almost entirely on the synthetic substitute. Most of the foreign exchange of Bangladesh is earned through its export of jute.

Rice is the staple food of Bengalees. Farmers have adopted dozens of rice varieties to meet local conditions. According to one estimate about 22 million acres of land is used to grow rice. For some of the reasons mentioned before, the yield per acre is very low. The Government of independent Bangladesh is taking steps to improve quality and quantity of rice per acre.

Little wheat is also grown. The leading areas where it is grown are Rajshahi, Rangpur, Kushtia, Pabna and Dacca.

Tea is an important earner of foreign exchange for Bangladesh. Bangladesh is seventh in rank in the production of tea. It is said that tea has been present in the Sylhet district since the ancient times. In those days, the natives used it in a different way. Its cultivation commenced around the year 1856. It is also said that coffee and cocoa were grown in Sylhet in the middle of the nineteenth century. It was later discovered that tea was profitable from a business point of view. Therefore cultivation of tea superseded coffee and cocoa. Ninety-five per cent of Bangladesh's total tea is grown in Sylhet. It is grown at Chittagong and Comilla districts as well.

Some historians have said that sugar-cane has been cultivated in the Bangladesh region since the ancient times. In the nineteenth century it was exported. Now it is used to produce sugar for the domestic consumption only. The climate of Bangladesh is suitable for its cultivation, as it is for jute and rice.

Some parts of Bangladesh are very suitable for the cultivation of tobacco. Before World War II, tobacco was exported to some neighbouring countries. Experiments have been successfully made to grow such foreign varieties of tobacco as, Virginia, Havana and Turkish. But these are not widely cultivated.

Various oil-seeds are grown, though not in large quantity. Mymensingh and the northern districts produce the most. There has been a sharp decline in the cultivation of cotton. It is grown around Chittagong Hill Tracts and Garo Hills and in some parts of Mymensingh. Also there is some cultivation of betelnuts and coconuts.

---

[5] J. C. Jack, *The Economic Life of a Bengal District* (Oxford, 1916), p. 38.

Plate 11—Hordes of refugees sheltering in cow sheds.

Plate 12—Refugees from Bangladesh receiving food and shelter in India.

18—INDUSTRIES

ONCE DACCA produced the finest quality muslin, which was in demand all over the world and particularly by the nobility of European countries. Today, it is no longer available, not even in the museum of Dacca. Its historical model could be seen in the national museum of Delhi, India. It was from the nineteenth century that the muslin industry began to deteriorate. The British imperialist policy which was largely dictated by its own interests was responsible for its deterioration.

Nowadays thousands of people in Bangladesh are engaged in handloom cotton-weaving industry. These people produce saris, towels, bed sheets, wrappers and so on. It is actually a cottage industry which is pursued side by side with farming, the main occupation of the villagers. Dacca, Pabna, Mymensingh, Noakhali and Bogra are the chief places where the cottage industry has flourished.

Jute is one of the major industries of Bangladesh. The partition of the sub-continent damaged this industry, both in West Bengal (India) and in Bangladesh. While most of the jute is produced in Bangladesh, its processing is done in West Bengal. The processing mills in West Bengal remained in constant demand for raw material, because the Pakistan Government had banned trade between both the countries. As a result of this ban, Bangladesh and West Bengal suffered heavily. After independence, Bangladesh established trade relations with India. About 20 per cent of Bangladesh's population is employed in the jute industry. The country has about twenty mills, most of which are concentrated at Narayanganj, Chittagong and Khulna.

Bangladesh is an ideal place for the cotton industry, because the country has cheap and plentiful labour and warm and moist climate. But this industry, for lack of raw material, never progressed. At the time of India's partition, Bangladesh had only ten cotton factories, later a few more were added. Still these factories have not been able to produce enough thread to meet the domestic demand. The cotton industry is concentrated at Narayanganj, Dacca, Kushtia and Khulna.

The forests have given rise to some industries; some of these concern timber. Some kinds of timber are used for match-sticks, for match-boxes, posts, railway sleepers, ships, electric poles, boats, etc. The country has about twenty match factories. Some kinds of woods, namely bamboo, are used to make paper. Karnajuli has a large paper mill, and near Khulna there is a large news-print factory.

The country has a few small food-processing plants such as for rice, sugar, tea and oil-seeds. Some small factories are about hides, skins and rubber goods. The government has set up a car plant at Chittagong; the plant turns out about 2,000 cars a year. At present, nearly 70 per cent of its parts are imported.

19—LANGUAGE AND LITERATURE

BENGALI belongs to the Eastern Prakrit group of the family of the Indo-Aryan languages. It is one of the oldest languages of the sub-continent and among the thirteen world languages which are spoken by more than fifty million people. It is a mother tongue of around 133 million Bengalees out of which sixty million live in West Bengal, India, and the rest of them in Bangladesh. As far as literary or standard Bengali is concerned, it is one throughout Bangladesh and West Bengal. At certain places its dialects have come into existence. For instance in Bangladesh, the dialect spoken at Chittagong and Sylhet are different from the language of the rest of the country. Being one of the oldest languages, Bengali received time and opportunity to develop and flourish and therefore its literature became rich, especially in poetry.

The earliest Bengali literature available now was written around the 7th century. The religious rites and cult have been the source of its medieval literature. In the 16th century, Allauddin Hossain, a ruler of Bengal from Arabia, patronized Bengali and thus assisted to develop the language further. It is said that translation of two famous Hindu epics, *Ramayana* and *Mahabharta,* into Bengali were arranged by a Muslim ruler.

The modern Bengali literature begins from the early part of the 19th century. Around this time, the British brought Bengal under its complete control. The growing power of the British in India affected the local languages. Influenced by the English language and literature the Bengalee writers began to think differently. Isvar Chandra Viddiya Sagar, Bankim Chandra, Michael Madhusudhan Detta, Meer Mushrraf Hossain and Kaikobad are some of the leading literary figures of this era.

Rabindranath Tagore started his literary career in the 19th century and continued it till 1941 when he died. The prolific genius of Tagore was recognized when he was awarded the Nobel Prize in literature in 1913. The Bangladesh Government has honoured him by adopting one of his poems as the national anthem. Sarat Chandra, Prabhat Kumar and Bibhuti Bhushan are outstanding literary contemporaries of Rabindranath Tagore.

Kazi Nazrul Islam started his writing when Tagore was still alive, and continued writing long after Tagore's death. He is considered a rebel poet, because he wrote against the British rule, and to sympathize the oppressed and the haves-not. Though a Muslim, Kazi Nazrul Islam never accepted the ideology of Pakistan and that is why the Pakistan Government never accepted him. But the people of Bangladesh as well as of West Bengal, India, have recognized his genius. Apart from poetry, he wrote plays, novels and short stories. Among his contemporaries the names of Dr. Mohammad Shahidullah, Suniti Kumar, Tarashanker, Sudhindranath Dutta, Shukanta, Jibanananda Das, Dr. Enamul Haq and of professor Abdul Hye could be included. The list of the most recent writers could consist of Sufia Kamal, Jashimuddin, Abul Fazal, Ahsan Habib, Sayed Walliullah, Shankatosman, Munir Chowdhury, Shamsur Rahman, Hasan Hafizur Rahman, Syed Shamsul Haq, Zahir Raihan, Sanaul Haq and Abdul

Gaffar Chowdhury. At the wake of independence of Bangladesh many writers and artists attempted themes concerning atrocities committed by Pakistani soldiers on Bengalees.

After the partition of the sub-continent in 1949, Pakistan tried to annihilate culture, language and literature of Bangladesh. There were attempts to make people consider Rabindranath Tagore as an alien writer, though without much success. Soon after the formation of Pakistan, Mr. Mohammad Ali Jinnah made it clear to Bengalees that Urdu will be the lingua franca of Pakistan and whosoever will mislead the people on this issue will be an enemy of the country. This decision of Pakistani rulers was based on the assumption that Urdu is an Islamic language because its script is similar to that of the Arabic and Persian languages. The listeners were deeply disturbed when Mr. Jinnah declared Urdu as the state language at the Dacca University Convocation in March 1948. Later, they arranged demonstrations against the government's decision and consequently many of them were arrested.

Around that time the government initiated a movement to introduce Arabic script into the Bengali language. On the 26th of January 1952, the whole of Bangladesh was enraged with the government's policy concerning its language. The students observed strike and arranged meetings and demonstrations. On the 21st of February 1952, the atmosphere grew tenser which led to violence. A few students of Dacca University were killed by the police firing. When the Assembly meeting about the budget was being held, students were being shot by the policemen outside. The students got hold of a microphone and spoke loudly about the violence. This disturbed the Assembly's meeting. Many members of the ruling party as well as others came out of the Assembly to protest against the government's fierce step taken against the sympathizers of the Bengali language. The news of the killings spread like a wild fire. In Dacca there was a complete strike everywhere.

Later, a procession of about a million people was taken out. It led to more violence. The next day the angry mob burnt the office of a Muslim League newspaper called *Morning News*. The mob attempted to destroy the office of *Sangbad,* another Muslim League newspaper. But the troops arrived on time to open fire to save the office. After a three-day battle the government arrested a number of students, professors and other political leaders who backed the Bengalee people's demand for the recognition of their language as the state language.

A few incidents mentioned above manifest the Pakistan government's firm resolution to curb language and literature of Bengalees. Due to these and many more repressive measures, Bangladesh could not produce literary figures of international status. Since the country is now free it is hoped that it will produce eminent writers.

20—TWO FASCINATING TRIBES—BEDEH AND MORANG

BANGLADESH is fascinating for overseas visitors in many aspects, some of which relate to the country's primitive tribes. Two of these tribes deserve special mention for their quaint mode of life. The Bedeh is one of them.

The Bedehs are actually sea gypsies, unlike the desert gypsies who travel on camels along with the stuff of their daily need. The Bedehs spend their whole life in boats which as a matter of fact are their homes. Three-quarters of every boat is covered with a roof and is divided into cabins of different sizes. In the medium and large size cabins they keep their clothes and provisions to protect them from the rains. The rest of the cabins are used for the daily activities of the family. One of them is converted into the kitchen, by drilling a hole in its roof for the smoke to go out. In the boat's yard, children play and the men fish.

The Bedehs are usually snake charmers. In Bengali language the word Bedeh means the one who catches snakes. At a river's bank they catch snakes whose venom they use as an antidote against snakebite. They go from place to place and village to village, showing their snakes and feats of skill. Normally they select a roadside or a shady tree where they spread a small carpet and let one or two snakes creep in front of them. They keep blowing a pipe till a crowd gathers around them. Then they take out different kinds of snakes from their pots, informing spectators about each of them. Sometimes they also sell herbs. People give them money, rice and clothes for the snake shows or in exchange of herbs.

The Bedehs live in villages, consisting of twenty to thirty boats which they move from one place to another. Every village has its own chief who owns the largest boat. The chief settles their disputes, punishes culprits, and orders his tribesmen to move or stay at a place. The punishment is often in the form of cash payment. The chief's word is law for the rest.

The chief also arranges marriages among his tribesmen. Before the wedding, the groom gives a few clothes and silver ornaments to his bride. The Bedehs stop their boats beside a river bank to perform the simple marital rites on the bank, after that the groom takes his bride in a new boat, made by him before the marriage.

The Bedeh women are remarkably active and healthy. Every morning, they cook food for the whole family, and after that they go to the towns along with their snakes. Some of them sell ordinary diamonds, silver ornaments and medicines which they prepare from jungle herbs. They are famous among the illiterate people, especially the villagers, for their medications for toothache and back-ache. The villagers buy these medicines happily from them. Many Bedehs pretend to be witch doctors and as such have a thriving business among many superstitious Bengalees.

The Bedeh women are very talkative. During the snake shows they normally keep singing. They return to their boats at the usual time in the evening. During the day, the men look after the children, play on a musical instrument or catch fish. Sometimes, they accompany their wives when a show of cobra is to be performed.

Many Bedehs call themselves Muslims, but Muslims

deny them as such because the snake holds an important position in the Bedeh creed. Hindu Bedehs worship Manasa, the goddess of snakes.

The Bedehs are well known for their courage and bravery. Even in terrible storms and weathers they cross the mighty rivers without any fear. Their children learn to swim and to play with snakes at the age of two. The Bedehs' entire life is spent in boats and they are excellent sailors.

The Morangs belong to the Mongol stock. From the point of civilization, the Morangs are hundreds of years back, though they live close to the world of today. Their needs are simple and few, most of which they produce themselves. Their houses, boxes, cups and glasses are made from the bamboo, and many of their utensils from the gourd.

About twenty thousand people of the Morang tribe live around the mountainous Chittagong which is covered with thick jungles and is intersected by numerous large and small rivers. Sometimes, one has to cross thirty rivulets in a three-mile distance.

The Morangs believe rigidly in the division of labour. Their men farm, repair houses, make carpets, baskets, and milk cows. Their women prepare food for the family, take produce to the market to sell, and do ordinary household works. Before sowing, they collect grass in the fields and put it to fire. The next day, they sow different kinds of crops simultaneously in the same field.

The Morangs consider a marriage successful, if the bride is older than the groom. They maintain that the wives who are older than their mates can manage their homes efficiently. Before wedding, the bachelors of the tribe often visit the homes of the girls of their choice and have complete freedom to meet them, even in the presence of their elders. This custom is unusual for the culture of the sub-continent. On the wedding day, the groom elopes with his bride. Later, both go to the home of the bride's parents where the groom is asked to pay a price to wed their daughter. If this price is very high, the groom invites the elders of the tribe to settle the disagreement. If the verdict of the elders goes in favour of the groom, the bride's parents have to pay a fine and vice versa. The bridal gown is like a long loose cloth with which the girl wraps her whole body. The bride's cheeks and forehead are marked with several tiny coloured dots, and her lips and teeth are coloured pink. She wears bangles, bracelets and a necklace of beads.

The Morang men are strong and muscular, have long hair and wear turbans. The youths decorate their ears with flowers of different hues. Many Morangs have become Buddhists. Still there are many who do not follow any particular religion. Their creed consists of superstitions and old traditions. The Morangs live according to their tribal customs and have passion for music and dance. On certain occasions, a man with a big drum would sit amidst men and women. As he initiates his drum beats, the crowd follow him with the tribal dance. The girls put on ankle rings which produce music as their feet move to the beats of the drum. The old people also attend these functions. At its conclusion, normally a cow is butchered to feed the people.

Rice is the staple food, as it is for the rest of the Bengalees. Due to over-eating, most of the men have fat, bulging bellies. Their average age is said to be very high. They use herbs and the services of witch doctors when they are ill.

The Morangs have their own councils to handle their disputes. They approach the government only when a severe disaster such as a famine or flood afflicts them.

They keep a dead body for seven days in the house. On the eighth day, the dead body is burnt on a river's bank. Its ashes are preserved in a box which is later buried.

21—POLITICAL PERSONALITIES

*　　　*　　　*

HUSSAIN SHAHEED SUHRAWARDY

HUSSAIN SHAHEED SUHRAWARDY was born in Midnapur in 1883, and received his early education at Calcutta Madrasah and St. Xavier's College. Later, he attended Oxford University where he obtained his degrees of M.A. and B.C.L. He was called to the Bar from Gray's Inn.

Suhrawardy's entire life was associated, in one way or another, with the national politics. In his early days, he became the Deputy Mayor of Calcutta Corporation. He held portfolios of Minister of Labour, Finance, Public Health and Local Self-Government in turn in the Bengal Assembly. Gradually, he rose to the position of Chief Minister. Once, he acted as Secretary of the Muslim League of Bengal province. During all these days, prior to the partition, he supported vehemently the Muslim League's demand for Pakistan.

After India's partition, he organized and convened the Jinnah Awami League in Pakistan. He joined the Central Cabinet on the 20th of December 1954, and in June 1955 he was elected to the East Pakistan Constituent Assembly on the Awami League's ticket. He held the position of Prime Minister for a term. During his term of office, he visited China on a goodwill mission.

Suhrawardy was the first Muslim League leader to realize the absurdity of the demand for a separate state for the Indian Muslims. From the eve of the partition of the sub-continent he began to demand a sovereign state for the whole Bengal province. After the creation of Pakistan, he came under the influence of Mahatma Gandhi whom he often visited and from whom he sought advice on certain matters. Consequently, Suhrawardy began to be considered as a traitor by such West Pakistani leaders as Liaquat Ali Khan. Mr. Jyoti Sen Gupta writes that "in private discussions with me, he (Suhrawardy) often claimed that it was he who created Pakistan. The Congress would never have bended down to accept the partition of India and the creation of Pakistan had there been no Calcutta killings in the 'Direct Action'. Mr. Suhrawardy regretted the killings but owned the authorship of the carnage which, he thought, forced the Congress to accept the division of the country."[6]

*　　　*　　　*

KHWAJA NAZIMUDDIN

Khwaja Nazimuddin was born on the 19th of July 1894, to an orthodox feudal family of the Nowabs of Dacca. His ancestors came from Kashmire. For higher education, Khwaja Nazimuddin attended the Aligarh Muslim University, India, and Cambridge University, England.

From 1930 to 34, he was the Minister for Education of Bengal; and from 1937 to 41, he was the Home Minister of the same province. He became a member of the Defence Committee of the Muslim League in 1942,

---

[6]Jyoti Sen Gupta, *Eclipse of East Pakistan* (Calcutta, 1963), p. 16.

and of the Committee of Direct Action in 1946. He formed the first Muslim League Ministry in Bengal in 1943, which lasted for two years.

After the partition of India, he was offered the position of the Chief Minister of East Pakistan. It was said that he was considered for this position because he owed allegiance to the British rule, who knighted him for his services rendered to the Crown, and because he was against Suhrawardy. The government under Khwaja Nazimuddin did nothing to reduce the agrarian problems nor did it draw plans to check the rapidly deteriorating unemployment situation. Since he had blood ties with other landed aristocracy he did not take steps to bring about land reforms. In February 1952, when he was the Prime Minister of Pakistan, he spoke once in favour of Urdu, which resulted in bloody violence in Dacca. For his lenient attitude towards the Muslim League, many Bengalees began to hate him.

After Mohammad Ali Jinnah's death, Nazimuddin was raised to the position of Pakistan's Governor-General. At that time Liaquat Ali Khan was the Prime Minister of the country. After Liaquat Ali's assassination, Khwaja Nazimuddin became the Prime Minister. On the 10th of April 1953, when he was the Prime Minister, he announced at a press conference that the country was facing a serious famine. Seven days after this announcement, the Governor-General, Mr. Ghulam Mohammad, called Nazimuddin and his ministers to his residence and dismissed them all on the grounds that they failed to perform their duties. Khwaja Nazimuddin attempted to solicit the help of the Queen by telephone, but failed to get connection. It was felt in a circle of politicians that the Governor-General took this step on the advice of the U.S. State Department.

Mr. Nazimuddin loved hunting and fishing, and was a

patron of wrestling and boxing tournaments, and of football, hockey and cricket matches. He was fond of rich and varied Moghul style dishes.

*   *   *

FAZLUL HAQ

Fazlul Haq, son of an advocate of Calcutta High Court, was born at Chakhar village in Barisal in 1873. He attended the Presidency College, Calcutta, after receiving his early education at the Barisal High School. He obtained his law degree and a master's degree in mathematics from Calcutta University.

For sometime he taught at a college, and later served as a Deputy Magistrate. On the advice of Nowab Salimullah he entered politics to unite the Muslims to demand the partition of India. Politically, he became a spokesman of the educated Bengalee Muslims. He resigned from government service to establish his own legal practice in Calcutta. He served as an elected member on the Bengal Legislative Council, the Reformed Bengal Council, and the Indian Legislative Assembly, on different occasions. He was the Secretary of the Bengal Provincial Muslim League from 1913 to 1916, and the President of the All-India Muslim League from 1916 to 1921. He was appointed as Education Minister of Bengal province in 1924. After two years he founded the Krishak Praja Party of which he ever remained a president. He represented the Bengalee Muslims at the first Round Table Conference which was held in November 1930, in London. He was elected as Mayor of Calcutta in 1935, and held the position of Bengal's Chief Minister from the 1st of April 1937 to the 28th of March 1943.

Fazlul Haq is one of the architects of Pakistan. He is

111

the one who moved the historical Pakistan Resolution at the All-India Muslim League conference held in Lahore in 1940. He moved to Dacca after the partition of the sub-continent. In Pakistan, he emerged as a strong politician. He took a lead in forcing the Muslim League Government to hold democratic elections. In 1951, the Pakistan Government made him Advocate-General of the east wing, now Bangladesh. He soon resigned this position to take up the leadership of the opposition against the Muslim League. The Bengalee Muslims rejoiced at his appearance in the political field, hailing him as "Sher-E-Bengal", which means the Bengal's lion.

On the 23rd of September 1953, in a meeting at his residence, he formed the Krishak Sramik Party. After a few months he constituted the United Front, which consisted of all the opposition parties. To assure Fazlul Haq the post of the Chief Minister, the United Front elected him its leader. Consequently, he formed the United Front's Ministry on the 3rd of April 1954. His government faced a hostile central government. He was detained under house arrest on the 19th of May 1954, under the charges that he sought freedom for his region by seeking help from communists and Indian agents. For six months he remained in his room. He was not allowed to see anyone, except his close relations.

Perhaps, Fazlul Haq was the only political leader of his time who was popular and commanded respect of all classes of people. He was much loved by the peasants.

*　　　*　　　*

SHEIKH MUJIBUR RAHMAN

Sheikh Mujibur Rahman was born on the 17th of March 1920, in Tongipara village of East Bengal, to a

112

Plate 13—Mukti Fauj soldiers in a trench.

Plate 14—Crowd, carrying Indian Commander, rejoicing on liberation of Burichang.

middle-class Muslim landowner's family. He received his early education at a mission school, and obtained his B.A. degree from Islamia College of Calcutta. Later, he joined Dacca University to study law. Around those days he developed a taste for the writings of Rabindranath Tagore, and of George Bernard Shaw.

From his childhood Mujib bore an antipathy to the British rule in India. When he was in the seventh grade he was jailed for six days for his demonstrations in favour of India's independence. At the university he supported a strike of the university menial workers for which he was imprisoned and then expelled from the university. In his youth, before the partition of India, he was an active student leader of the All-India Muslim League. Once he was elected to the Council of the All-India Muslim Students Federation, and later to the Muslim League. After the partition he severed his ties with the Muslim League and began to fight for the autonomy of his region. He was jailed the first time after the formation of Pakistan in 1948, when he resisted imposition of Urdu as Pakistan's national language. He was sentenced to three years imprisonment in 1949 because he participated in illegal strikes and demonstrations against the Pakistan Government. He emerged a very popular leader of the Bengalees after his release from jail. He became a key member of the newly organized East Pakistan's party, called the Awami League, and was elected to the provincial assembly.

Sheikh Mujibur Rahman assumed a powerful role as an opposition leader when Field-Marshal Ayub Khan established his military dictatorship in 1958. Mujib's activities again resulted in his imprisonment in 1958 and in 1962.

In 1966, Sheikh Mujib launched his six-point programme to give the provinces control over taxation, foreign aid, and foreign trade, leaving defence and some aspects of foreign relations with the central government. Ayub Khan had him arrested on the grounds that he plotted to achieve independence for East Pakistan. A widespread opposition to Ayub Khan compelled him to free Mujib and to resign.

The next dictator of Pakistan, General Yahya Khan, put Sheikh Mujib in jail on the same charges. He arrested Mujib at his home at Dacca, on the night of the 26th of March 1971. After a few days, Mujib was taken to West Pakistan, where he was tried by a military court. Many newspapers reported the possibility of Mujib's having been killed by the military and that the trial was a hoax to cover his secret execution. This suspicion gained strength because Mujib's trial was kept a top secret and he was not allowed to have a lawyer, except a Pakistani whom he refused to have. It was also reported that he was detained in an unfurnished jail without electricity and water. Mujib's arrest led many world leaders to appeal to the Pakistani Government to handle his case leniently.

Sheikh Mujib was tried by the military regime for waging war against Pakistan. This charge carried a penalty of death or life imprisonment. As the proceedings of the trial ended, Pakistan became involved in a grim armed conflict with India. The military became busy with the war preparation and the penalty was never announced. Mujib was taken to a jail in Mianwali, the home of K. M. Niazi who commanded the Pakistan forces in the east. Nearly all the prisoners of this jail were the residents of Mianwali. The prisoners were told that Niazi had been killed by the Bengalees and incited to retaliate by killing Mujib. Two hours before the plot could be executed, the superintendent of the jail, a friendly man, took Mujib to his residence. After a few days he began to fear that Mujib's disappearance from the jail was going to be disclosed. In order to be cautious, he hid Mujib in an unoccupied house several

114

miles away from his home. Mujib remained there for nine days.

When Bhutto came to power he announced his desire to see Mujib. Consequently, he was taken to Rowalpindi where he was put under house arrest in a guest house. Bhutto met Mujib three times, always with the same purpose of asking him to find some way to link again, though loosely, both the wings of Pakistan. Sheikh Mujib refused to give any assurance without the consultation of his people. After Mujib's total imprisonment of ten months, Bhutto sent him to London in a chartered flight on the 8th of January 1972. The arrangements of the flight were made under strict security guard. Mujib told at a news conference in London that as he had been under the sentence of death, he was kept in a condemned man's cell. The intense heat and the solitary confinement were hard to bear. From the noise of the aeroplanes he figured out that Pakistan was engaged in a war, but he did not know the war's results until Bhutto informed him about it. After an overnight's stay in London, Mujib came to Dacca, where he was greeted with shouts of joy by half a million Bengalees.

Sheikh Mujib has spent nine years and eight months in jail, more than any political leader of Bangladesh. He is grey-haired, stocky and six feet tall, and wears normally a loose white shirt with a black, sleeveless jacket. He has an uncanny ability to remember names and faces. As an orator he is spellbinding; his style is pungent and fervent.

Mujib is moderately pro-western, and is keen to establish good neighbourly and trade relations with India. His political views are moderate. He could be called a social democrat, because he believes in the nationalization of key industries. During his imprisonment in Pakistan, he was called President of Bangladesh by his followers. After the formation of the Bangladesh Government he took over as the Prime Minister on the 12th of January 1972.

*   *   *

SYED NAZRUL ISLAM

Syed Nazrul Islam was born in the Jashodal village of the Mymensingh district of Bangladesh in 1925. He obtained his master's degree from Dacca University. After serving for a year in the Taxation Department, he taught at Ananda Mohan College, Mymensingh. In 1951 he joined the Mymensingh Bar.

Nazrul Islam has been taking an active part in politics since his university days. He was the Vice-President of Salinullah Muslim Hall Students Union and a member of the All-Party Action Committee. In those days the movement concerning the demand for the recognition of Bengali as a state language was very strong. He was one of the motivating spirits behind this movement.

In 1949, when Sheikh Mujibur Rahman, the Awami League's leader, was arrested in connection with the "Agartala Conspiracy Case", Syed Nazrul Islam organized the Democratic Action Committee which succeeded in arousing such an outcry that Ayub Khan was compelled to withdraw the case. He stood firmly against the autocratic rule of Ayub Khan, demanding democracy. In 1966, when Mujib and other leaders were arrested, Nazrul Islam led his countrymen in the role of Acting President of the Awami League.

In 1970 he was elected to the National Assembly and was chosen for the position of Deputy Leader of the Awami League Parliamentary Party. After the military crackdown on the 25th of March 1971 he went underground, but still led his people. On the 17th of April he

formed the government of the People's Republic of Bangladesh. During those troubled days he served his country
as the Acting-President of Bangladesh.

Syed Nazrul Islam has a cool and commanding per-
sonality, and is a powerful speaker. He was sworn in as
Minister of Industries, Trade and Commerce of the
Mujib Cabinet on the 12th of January 1972.

*   *   *

ABU SAYED CHOWDHURY

Mr. Justice Abu Sayed Chowdhury graduated from the
Presidency College, Calcutta, India and obtained his
degrees of M.A. and B.L. from the University of Calcutta. For higher legal studies he went to England and
was called to the Lincoln's Inn in 1947.

Mr. Chowdhury was appointed Advocate-General of
East Pakistan in March 1960. As a member of the constitution commission headed by Mr. Justice M. Shaha-
buddin, he contributed to the framing of the Pakistan's
constitution. He was appointed an additional judge of
Dacca High Court on the 7th of July 1961, and was
made a permanent judge on the 22nd of November 1962.
He was also chairman of the Central Board for the development of Bengali language.

In November 1969, Mr. Chowdhury was appointed
Vice-Chancellor of Dacca University for four years. He
was appointed to serve as Pakistan's representative on the
U.N. Commission on Human Rights in January 1971.
Mr. Chowdhury declared his allegiance to the Government of Bangladesh soon after the Pakistani army
crackdown on the 25th of March 1971 while he was
proceeding to attend a conference of the U.N. Commission
on Human Rights on behalf of Pakistan.

He worked as Ambassador-at-large for the Bangladesh Government with headquarters in London and returned when the country was free. He was sworn in as President of Bangladesh on the 12th of January 1972.

*   *   *

TAJUDDIN AHMED

Tajuddin Ahmed was born in a village of Dacca district in 1925. He obtained his bachelor's degree in Economics from the University of Dacca, and his law degree from the same university while he was a political prisoner.

When he was in his early forties he was drawn to the Muslim League politics. In 1944 he was elected to the Bengal Council of the Muslim League. Soon after the partition of India, he disassociated himself from the Muslim League, assuming leadership of students. He took a leading part in the movement of the students to compel the government to recognize Bengali as a state language. He joined the Awami League in 1949; since that time he has been serving the party in different capacities. He was Secretary-General of the Dacca District Awami League from 1953 to 1957. In 1955 he was elected to the position of Social and Cultural Secretary of the Provincial Awami League. In 1964, he became the Organizing Secretary and in 1966, the party's Secretary-General. He was arrested when the Ayub Khan regime attempted to destroy the Awami League's movement based on a six-point programme. During the 1970-71 elections he served as Secretary of the Awami League Parliamentary Board. He was returned to the National Assembly by an overwhelming majority during the 1970 general elections.

The Pakistan military tried its best to arrest him after its crackdown on the 25th of March 1971, but he cleverly escaped the military's grasp. The military tried him in absentia and sentenced him to fourteen years rigorous imprisonment. Besides, his home was ransacked and his property confiscated. Somehow, he managed to group together the elected members and the party workers to decide about the future course of action. In April 1971, when the Independent Republic of Bangladesh was proclaimed, he was sworn in as Prime Minister of the country. As Prime Minister, he built up the machinery of the Bangladesh Government from scratch in the face of enormous difficulties and hardships. On the 10th of January 1972, he was sworn in as Minister for Finance, Planning and Revenue in Sheikh Mujib's Cabinet.

Tajuddin Ahmed first met Sheikh Mujib in Calcutta in 1944 and since then there has grown a deep political understanding between them. These days he is one of the outstanding politicians of Bangladesh.

THE GOVERNMENT OF PEOPLE'S REPUBLIC OF BANGLADESH

Members of the Cabinet

President:	Sheikh Mujibur Rahman
Vice-President:	Syed Nazrul Islam
Prime Minister:	Mr. Tajuddin Ahmad
Minister. In Charge of Foreign Affairs, Law and Parliamentary Affairs:	Khandaker Moshtaque Ahmed
Minister. In Charge of Finance, Commerce and Industries:	Mr. M. Mansoor Ali
Minister. In Charge of Interior, Supply, Relief and Rehabilitation:	Mr. A. H. M. Kamruzzaman

PART III

BANGLADESH DIGEST

___

22—SOME BASIC FACTS

AGRICULTURE
  Bangladesh is primarily an agricultural country. The total land under cultivation is 22,429,865 acres. The main crops are : rice, jute, tea, sugar-cane, tobacco, wheat, and various oil seeds.

AIR-PORTS
  Dacca, Chittagong, Jessore, Essordy, Sylhet, Comilla, Coicaser Bazaar.

AREA
  55,127 square miles.

BOUNDARY
  North : West Bengal and Assam (India).
  South : Bay of Bengal and Burma.
  East : Assam (India) and Burma.
  West : West Bengal and Bihar (India).

CAPITAL
  Dacca.

CLIMATE
  The country has a typical tropical monsoon climate with warm wet summer and cool dry winter.

FORESTS
Forests comprise 16.12 per cent of the total area of the country.

INCOME
Income per capita hovers around 75 dollars per year.

INDUSTRIES
Jute, sugar, paper, textile, cement, newsprint.

IMPORTANT PLACES
Chalna, Chittagong, Cox's Bazar, Dacca, Khulna, Mongla, Mymensingh, Narayanganj, Rajshahi, Sylhet.

LOCATION
Between $20° -30'$ and $26° -45'$ North Latitude and $92° -56'$ East Longitude.

NATIONAL FLOWER
White water lily (Shapla in Bengali).

OFFICIAL LANGUAGE
Bengali.

OFFICIAL NAME
The People's Republic of Bangladesh.

POPULATION
Seventy-five million. The country ranks eighth among the world's 148 nations in terms of population. Density of population is 3,000 persons per square mile.

RAINFALL
The average annual rainfall varies from 50 inches to 200 inches.

RELIGIONS
Muslims, Hindus, Buddhists and Christians. About 85 per cent of the population is Muslim.

SEAPORTS
Chalna, Chittagong, Kakaz Bazar, Mongla.

UNIVERSITIES
Chittagong, Dacca, Mymensingh, Rajshahi.

23—CHRONOLOGY OF IMPORTANT DATES

June 20, 1947   The members of the Bengal Assembly decide to partition the province.

August 25, 1947   The food situation becomes serious in East Pakistan due to floods.

March 11, 1948   Sheikh Mujibur Rahman is arrested while leading a language demonstration.

August 14, 1948   Khwaja Nazimuddin, the Chief Minister of East Pakistan, is appointed Governor-General of Pakistan.

November 24, 1950   Thirteen Bengalee members of the Muslim League Assembly Party demand internal autonomy for East Pakistan.

February 21, 1952   Demonstrations are held to demand the recognition of Bengali as a state language. Nineteen students and some other people are killed by the police firing.

March 19, 1954   The United Front led by Fazlul Haq wins the provincial elections with a thumping majority.

124

April 3, 1954   Fazlul Haq forms the United Front Ministry.

May 15, 1954   The riots between Bengalees and non-Bengalees break out at Adamjee Jute Mill in Narayanganj. Over 600 persons are killed and many hundreds are wounded.

May 19, 1954   Fazlul Haq is detained under house arrest under the charges that he sought freedom for his region with the help of communists and Indian agents. He remains in his room for six months.

August 4, 1954   Millions of people are affected by floods.

October 7, 1958   President Iskander Mirza imposes Martial Law across Pakistan.

October 12, 1958   Sheikh Mujibur Rahman, Maulana Bhashani and Khan Abdul Ghaffar Khan are arrested.

October 27, 1958   Field-Marshal Mohammad Ayub Khan forces Iskander Mirza to quit his office. Ayub Khan assumes the country's reign and imposes Martial Law.

October 26, 1959   President Ayub Khan announces his scheme for the basic democracy.

September 12, 1960   Mujibur Rahman is convicted in Dacca on the charge of criminal misconduct and is sentenced to two years imprisonment.

October 10, 1960   A cyclone hits the coastal belt of East Pakistan. More than 3,000 people are killed.

October 31, 1960   Another cyclone kills 20,000 persons

and render numerous homeless.

May 9, 1961 — Another cyclone hits East Pakistan. Two thousand persons are killed and many thousands become homeless.

September 21, 1961 — Students in Dacca demonstrate against Ayub Khan. Hundreds of students are arrested.

September 24, 1961 — Hussain Shaheed Suhrawardy demands the restoration of democracy.

April, 1962 — More demonstrations are held against Ayub Khan. Many people are killed by the police firing. Four Bengalee members of the Central Cabinet resign to protest against Ayub's repressive measures.

June 9, 1962 — Martial Law is lifted. A new constitution based on "Basic Democracy" is introduced. The people of East Pakistan oppose the constitution.

September 12, 1962 — At Dacca, the students organize a massive demonstration against the Central Government's decision to lengthen the duration of the B.A. degree course by one year. Students are forbidden to participate in politics.

September 17, 1962 — The students call for protest meetings and a general strike. The military is called in to disperse the demonstrators. Two persons are killed and about two hundred are wounded by the bullets fired by

126

	the soldiers. Ayub Khan dismisses the Vice-Chancellor of Dacca University on the grounds that he could not control the students' activities.
July 1, 1964	Ayub Khan compels the educational institutions to prohibit their teachers from participating in politics.
September 24, 1964	A huge strike is arranged to force the Government to release the political prisoners. The strike meets with a complete success.
September 6, 1965	Indo-Pak war breaks out in Kashmire.
February, 1966	Sheikh Mujibur Rahman announces his Six Points concerning regional autonomy.
March 20, 1966	Sheikh Mujib and some of his party workers are arrested. Ayub Khan denounces the autonomy movement.
June 7, 1966	A general strike is called to demand the release of the political prisoners. Anti-Ayub demonstrations are arranged across East Pakistan. Eleven persons are killed at various places by the firing of the police on demonstrators, and eight hundred workers are arrested.
February 2, 1967	The opposition leaders of East Pakistan form a united front for the realization of regional autonomy.
April 27, 1967	Sheikh Mujibur Rahman is sentenced to fifteen months imprisonment for making a speech.

127

January 5, 1968   The students of Dacca University arrange an exhibition to indicate the disparities between East Pakistan and West Pakistan.

January 18, 1968   Sheikh Mujibur Rahman is arrested on the charges that he tried to achieve independence of his region with the help of foreign agents.

July 18, 1968   Many districts of East Pakistan are hit by a cyclone. Thousands of people are killed and rendered homeless.

September, 1968   President Ayub Khan visits East Pakistan to convince the Bengalees that democracy was not suited to Pakistan. The Bengalees greet him with demonstrations and black flags.

October 10, 1968   Students launch anti-government agitation.

November 7, 1968   Abortive attempt to assassinate Ayub Khan.

December 7, 1968   Anti-Ayub demonstrations are held across East Pakistan. Many demonstrators are killed by the police firing. Five hundred persons are arrested.

December 14, 1968   More demonstrations are held against Ayub Khan and many more persons are jailed.

February 14, 1969   General strike across the country.

February 22, 1969   "Agartala Conspiracy Case" against Mujib and others is withdrawn.

March 25, 1969   Field-Marshal Ayub Khan resigns. General Yahya takes over the

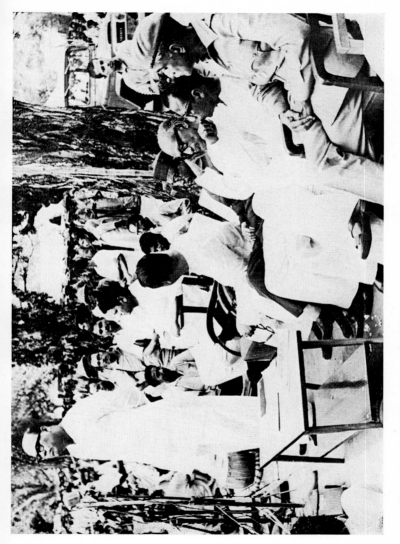

Plate 15—Syed Nazral Islam addressing a meeting at inauguration of Bangladesh.

Plate 16—President of Bangladesh Sheikh Mujibur Rahman addressing a meeting.

	charge and imposes Martial Law.
March 26, 1969	General Yahya Khan disclaims any political ambition. He assures the Bengalees the restoration of democracy.
March 30, 1969	Maulana Bhashani, the National Awami Party Chief, demands a national government.
April 10, 1969	General Yahya Khan pledges to hold elections on the basis of adult franchise.
November 28, 1969	Yahya Khan fixes the 5th of October 1970 for elections.
January 1, 1970	Political restrictions are lifted. The political parties resume full activities.
September 2, 1970	Elections are postponed until the 7th of December due to the cyclone in East Pakistan.
December 7, 1970	Elections to the National Assembly completed. The Awami League of Mujibur Rahman emerges the strongest political party of Pakistan.
December 9, 1970	Sheikh Mujib demands that the Constitution of Pakistan must be based on his Six Points of regional autonomy.
January 14, 1971	General Yahya Khan refers to Mujibur Rahman as Pakistan's future Prime Minister.
January 29, 1971	Mujibur Rahman and Z. A. Bhutto talk about the forthcoming constitution of Pakistan.
February 13, 1971	General Yahya Khan fixes the 3rd of

	March for the first session of the National Assembly.
February 15, 1971	Mr. Z. A. Bhutto announces that his party will boycott the National Assembly if Sheikh Mujib would not agree to frame constitution according to his views.
March 1, 1971	General Yahya Khan postpones indefinitely the Assembly session. Mujibur Rahman calls for general strike to protest against the postponement of the Assembly session.
March 2, 1971	Troops move into action. The curfew is imposed.
March 3, 1971	Non-violent, non-cooperation movement is launched under the direction of Sheikh Mujibur Rahman.
March 5, 1971	The army kills 300 Awami League volunteers and the people.
March 6, 1971	General Yahya Khan schedules the Assembly for the 25th of March.
March 7, 1971	Mujibur Rahman asks the people not to pay taxes, and asks Government servants to take orders from him. Mujib puts forth his four conditions for attending the Assembly session.
March 9, 1971	East Pakistan judges refuse to swear in Lt. Gen. Tikka Khan as Governor.
March 19, 1971	Talks concerning constitution begin between Yahya and Mujib, in Dacca.
March 21, 1971	Bhutto arrives in Dacca to join the Yahya-Mujib talks about the

constitution.

March 22, 1971   Yahya Khan postpones the inauguration of the National Assembly.

March 25, 1971   The Pakistan army attacks the unarmed Bengalees without giving
any warning. Sheikh Mujibur
Rahman is arrested. General Yahya Khan and Bhutto fly out of
Dacca.

March 26, 1971   General Yahya Khan bans all the
political activities, imposes com-
plete press censorship, closes all
educational institutions, termin-
ates all bank transactions and orders to freeze accounts. The world
begins to condemn the atrocities by
Pakistan army. Independence of
Bangladesh as a sovereign state is
declared on a radio.

April 10, 1971   The elected representatives of the
people of Bangladesh form a con-
stituent assembly, and confirm the
declaration of independence that
was made by Sheikh Mujibur Rahman. A cabinet is constituted with
Mujib as the President of the Republic of Bangladesh.

June 3, 1971   For the first time the U.N. Secretary-
General U. Thant expresses his
deep concern about the tragic
happenings in Bangladesh.

June 29, 1971   Senator Edward Kennedy urges the
U.S. Government to stop arms
shipment to Pakistan.

June 30, 1971   Canada embargos on arms shipment

	to Pakistan.
December 4, 1971	Indian troops cross into Bangladesh to help the Liberation Army.
December 6, 1971	India recognizes the Republic of Bangladesh.
December 7, 1971	Bhuttan recognizes Bangladesh.
December 16, 1971	Bangladesh is liberated completely. The Pakistan army surrenders to the joint command of the Bangladesh Liberation Forces and the Indian Armed Forces.
December 22, 1971	The Bangladesh Cabinet comes to Dacca from Mujibnagar.
January 10, 1972	Sheikh Mujibur Rahman returns home from London, via New Delhi, after his release from Pakistan prison.
January 11, 1972	German Democratic Republic recognizes Bangladesh.
January 12, 1972	Sheikh Mujibur Rahman is sworn in as the Prime Minister of the Government of the People's Republic of Bangladesh.

24—SELECTED BIBLIOGRAPHY

Ahmad, Nafis. *An Economic Geography of East Pakistan* (second edition). London : Oxford University Press, 1968.

Akhtar, Jamna Das. *The Saga of Bangla Desh.* Delhi : Oriental Publishers, 1971.

Ali, Chaudhri Muhammad. *The Emergence of Pakistan.* New York and London : Columbia University Press, 1967.

Bangabandhu Speaks (a collection of speeches and statements made by Sheikh Mujibur Rahman). The External Publicity Division, Ministry of Foreign Affairs, Government of Bangladesh.

Bangla Desh And Indo-Pak War. India : Ministry of Information and Broadcasting, 1972.

Bangla Desh: Contemporary Events and Documents. Bangladesh : The People's Republic of Bangla Desh.

Banerjee, D. N. *East Pakistan.* India : Vikas Publications, 1969.

"Between cloud nine and revolution," *The Economist,* April 1, 1972, pp. 38-39.

Binder, Leonard. *Religion and Politics in Pakistan.* Berkely and Los Angeles : University of California Press, 1961.

Chakravarty, Basudha. *Kazi Nazrul Islam.* New Delhi : National Book Trust, 1968.

"East Pakistan drives back the Jungles," *The National Geography Magazine,* March 1955, pp. 398-426.

Ellis, William S. "Bangladesh : Hope Nourishes a New Nation", *National Geographic,* September 1972, pp. 295-331.

Feldman, Herbert. *Pakistan—An Introduction.* Lahore, Karachi, Dacca : Oxford University Press, 1968.

Gankovsky, Y. V. and Gordon-Polonskaya, L. R. *A History of Pakistan.* Moscow : Nauka Publishing House, 1964.

Gupta, Jyoti Sen. *Eclipse of East Pakistan.* Calcutta : Renco, 1963.

"India : Easy Victory, Uneasy Peace", *Time* (Canada), December 27, 1971, pp. 20-22C.

Introducing Bangladesh. Bangladesh : External Publicity Division, Government of the People's Republic of Bangladesh, 1972.

Jack, J. C. *The Economic Life of a Bengal District.* Oxford : At the Clarendon Press, 1916.

134

SELECTED BIBLIOGRAPHY

"The Jute King", *Time* (Canada), 4 December 1964, p. 92.

Kazi, S. Ahmad. *A Geography of Pakistan*. Karachi, Lahore, Dacca : Oxford University Press, 1964.

Loshak, David. *Pakistan in Crisis*. New York : McGraw-Hill Book Company, 1971.

McCullum, Hugh. "Where Pakistanis die", *The Observer* (Canada), October 1971, p. 17.

"Pakistan: The Ravaging of Golden Bengal", *Time* (Canada), August 2, 1971, pp. 22-31.

"Rebellion in Bengla Desh", a pamphlet prepared by members of the Pacific Studies Center, 1963 University Avenue, East Polo Alto, California, May 7, 1971.

Richard and Exley, Helen (eds.). *The Testimony of Sixty*. Oxford : Oxfam, 1971.

Sarcar, Sanjib. *The Bleeding Humanity*. India : The Ecumenical Christian Centre, 1971.

Spear, Percival. *India*. U.S.A. : The University of Michigan Press, 1961.

Steinberg, S. H. (ed.). *The Statesman's Year Book 1968-69*. London, Melbourne, Toronto : Macmillan, 1968.

Symonds, Richard. *The Making of Pakistan*. London : Faber and Faber, 1950.

Tinker, Hugh. *India and Pakistan*. London : Pall Mall Press, 1962.

135

Trumbull, Robert. "Bengalis rebuilding quickly, but time is short", *The Montreal Star,* Wednesday, April 26, 1972.

"Vengeance in Victory", *Time* (Canada), January 3, 1972, pp. 31-32.

White Book on Bangla Desh. Finland : A World Peace Council Publication, 1972.

White Paper On The Crises In East Pakistan. Islamabad : Ministry of Information and National Affairs, Government of Pakistan, August 5, 1971.

Why Bangla Desh? Bangladesh : Public Relations Department, The People's Republic of Bangladesh.

Map 1—The Partition of India.

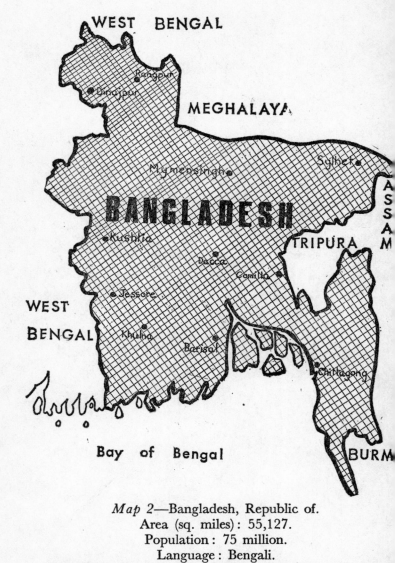

Map 2—Bangladesh, Republic of.
Area (sq. miles): 55,127.
Population: 75 million.
Language: Bengali.
Historical: Became a part of Pakistan in 1947. Declared itself a Sovereign Democratic Republic on 17 April, 1971.

26—INDEX

139

SO YOU WANT TO BE A VETERINARY SURGEON
R. S. Naismith, M.R.C.V.S.

Many people from Barristers to Barmen, Doctors to Dockers and Teachers to Tramps have confided in me that 'A Veterinary Surgeon is *really* what they would like to have been.' Circumstances of various kinds prevented fulfillment of this ambition in their lives.

Schoolboys and girls often ask about how to become a Veterinary Surgeon and this information is freely available from the Royal College of Veterinary Surgeons.

What is not so freely available is information on what it is like actually being a 'Vet' and that is what this book is also about — valuable information to help the school leaver.

The author is indebted to the help given to compiling this book by the Ministry of Agriculture, Royal Army Veterinary Corps, the Universities of Edinburgh, Glasgow, London, Liverpool, Dublin, Bristol and Cambridge, The World Health Organisation and the Veterinary Authorities of Canada, Australia, New Zealand, South Africa, Rhodesia and Kenya, as well as many colleagues who kindly gave information on their particular aspects of the Profession.

The author has freely drawn upon his own experiences from twenty-six years in general Practice.

Also the author expresses the hope that all who are interested in the work of the Veterinary Surgeon in his fight against the diseases of animals and his labours to make the world a better place for animals to live in, will get pleasure from reading this book and a greater understanding of that always busy and to some people 'mysterious' character "The Vet".

ISBN 0 85475 054 1   Illustrated

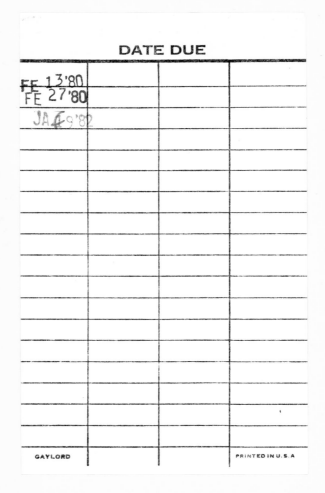

DATE DUE

FE 13'80			
FE 27'80			
JA 9'82			
GAYLORD			PRINTED IN U.S.A